D0421838

# BE HONEST

ALSO FROM 826 NATIONAL AND THE NEW PRESS

*Teachers Have It Easy: The Big Sacrifices and Small Salaries of America's Teachers*
by Daniel Moulthrop, Nínive Calegari, and Dave Eggers

# BE HONEST

*And Other Advice from Students Across the Country*

*Edited by* NÍNIVE CALEGARI

*with* MARIAMA LOCKINGTON

*and* LAURA McKINNEY

NEW YORK
LONDON

Published in the United States by The New Press, New York, 2011
Distributed by Perseus Distribution

LIBRARY OF CONGRESS CATALOGING-IN-PUBLICATION DATA
Be honest : and other advice from 826 students across the country /
edited by Nínive Calegari ; with Mariama Lockington and Laura McKinney.
p. cm.
ISBN 978-1-59558-609-4 (hc.)
1. Students—Conduct of Life. I. Calegari, Nínive Clements.
II. Lockington, Mariama. III. McKinney, Laura.
LB3609.B37 2011
371.8—dc22 2011012831

The New Press was established in 1990 as a not-for-profit alternative to the large, commercial publishing houses currently dominating the book publishing industry. The New Press operates in the public interest rather than for private gain, and is committed to publishing, in innovative ways, works of educational, cultural, and community value that are often deemed insufficiently profitable.

www.thenewpress.com

*Composition by dix!*

Printed in the United States of America

2 4 6 8 10 9 7 5 3 1

*This book is dedicated to young people's honesty and determination and to all the adults who have the courage to listen.*

# CONTENTS

# Preface

The students in this book have stuck their necks out. They have written honestly and courageously about their experiences in our classrooms all over the country. You will be moved by the tributes to teachers, entertained by the vignettes, and sometimes angered by the realities we ask our kids to face. When we talk about teaching and learning, we often divorce ourselves from the individual young people sitting in those seats. With this book, we hope to bring these individuals into the spotlight and to provide a microphone for their ideas and voices.

In the winter of 2002 I received a call from Kathleen Large, an English teacher at Leadership High School in San Francisco (where I had also taught). Kathleen had invited the entire eleventh-grade class to respond to James Baldwin's 1963 essay "Going for Broke." Leadership High was San Francisco's first charter school, and these students had a unique and powerful perspective—they were at the forefront of a significant educational reform in our country. Schools, teaching, learning, and policy were concepts the students understood well, questioned deeply, and discussed fluently. The students' responses encompassed everything from personal experiences to educational policies to teacher qualities that made them effective. Their essays were illuminating, and this was why Kathleen had called me. So, we decided to collect them into a book and publish the essays through 826 Valencia.

The next step was to bring 826 volunteers into the classrooms for several weeks. The tutors talked to the students about their work and gave them detailed feedback. The students, who had thought their work was finished, returned to their pieces and dedicated themselves to perfecting their words. All the students revised their work at least six more times to make sure the writing was honest, concise, insightful, and even inspiring. The essays then went to a student and tutor editorial board to edit, organize, and design the finished book.

*Talking Back: What Students Know About Teaching* was a huge success. The book was the first student-authored discussion of teaching and learning, and student teachers all over the country devoured it. We were thrilled by its popularity, and we're still extremely proud of those students and that book—826 National's first.

That project ended up laying the groundwork for all future 826 Young Author Books. We do this in all eight cities around the country where there are 826 chapters: A teacher generates a theme or idea for a book, and she tells us about her students. We then prepare dozens of volunteers and send them into her classroom to work one-on-one with the students for weeks, sometimes months. The students work harder than they've worked for any school assignment—revising and revising and revising. Students then volunteer to help shape and edit the book, learning every part of the editing and publishing process. We treat the students as professional authors and editors, providing honest feedback, rigorous standards, and appealing design. The book's publication is always celebrated with a party, and students proudly read to a large audience and autograph their work. The experience of becoming a published author can be transformative.

For the book you're holding in your hands, we expanded the topics we invited the students to write about and allowed students to select from among them. In these essays the student contributors designed their own schools, thanked their very best teachers with detailed letters, and wrote speeches in the voice of President Obama.

The students articulate what we need to hear: they want to be understood; they need and demand excellent, passionate teachers; they have important, life-molding experiences they are dying to share; they want rich, meaningful curricula; and finally, they want to be acknowledged by adults in an honest way—they want to feel proud of who they are, and they need the adults to help create the right atmosphere to make that happen.

What Kathleen Large wrote for the introduction to the original *Talking Back* remains relevant today: "It takes courage to ask young people to tell the truth; it takes humility to listen. The young people who wrote this book are good kids—really good—and all kids are good kids. Listen, those of you who figure yourselves as responsible, and go for broke."

The authors of *Be Honest* have succeeded again—their essays are insightful and heartfelt. You will enjoy them.

—Nínive Calegari
Co-founder of 826 Valencia and 826 National
January 2011

# Foreword: Pimp My Brain

Back when I was a kid, school was a mystery. Sometimes it worked, sometimes it didn't. I always assumed that was totally my own fault, and I was under the impression that I wasn't too bright. I didn't know the difference between perceived "intelligence" and "behavior." There was no evidence in my home life that made things any clearer, because I never saw my parents. I didn't understand why I was either ignored or in trouble—there seemed to be no happy medium. Why were those teachers so crazy about some stupid schoolbook when I was reading three to five books at home? Why was my attendance such a big deal? I took all my tests! I now understand that the real problem was that my teachers were expected to fill in for my parents, by everyone, from the president on down, but they were cutting budgets like mad and everyone was underwater. It was so unfair! They expected the teachers to work magic. In my heart I knew I was hard on my teachers, and as I got older I was even a little bitter. Knowing what I know now I realize they all deserve something better than that. I'm sad it was never brought to my attention that I needed to make an effort to understand them, too. I'm sorry, teachers!

What I love about this book is that we are here to write our collective letters to teachers, be it gushing praise, bittersweet regret, or plain old disappointment. It's a complicated relationship! We are also here to ask what we can do for those same teachers. We are here to make suggestions and celebrate the shared victories that our teachers made possible. We are here to ask your forgiveness and thank you for your patience, and to tell you a little about ourselves.

In my schools (I attended no fewer than ten, which probably makes me an expert) I rarely formed a fondness for any one teacher, but luckily, in the world of the late 1970s and early 1980s, there were still books. Thank goodness for books: they don't grade you, give you detention, or send you to the school shrink. They are quiet, exciting, life-changing friends. They are, in a pinch, *teachers*. Most of the time you couldn't get in trouble for reading one, either.

I remember learning how to cry out of one side of my face while reading *Where the Red Fern Grows* in the brown corduroy beanbag chairs in the library. I faced the cold library window—I couldn't let other people see me cry. That beautiful story, and a trillion others, made me feel so much, and my capacity for humanness and compassion grew and grew. My capacity for love grew, too, right along with my passion for books.

And strangely, books led me *to* a teacher rather than the other way around. That teacher's name was Mrs. Hughes. She was a very large middle-fifties lady who was continually mocked by the students—they called her "Mrs. Huge." She had small eyes and huge glasses. She wore out-of-date polyester pantsuits, and there was a large mole just under her thin, stiff bubble of cotton-candy hair. It was like a tiny bird's egg in a big wispy nest. One kid near me theorized that the mole was the button President Reagan would use to launch "The Bomb." (I sure don't miss the Cold War.) At first I laughed; there was no denying she was an easy target. The class only laughed until she made us read *The Outsiders* by S.E. Hinton. Man! Were we riveted! It was such an "adult" book in my mind, and it was about poor kids, like me, with no real parents or safety. Every kid in the class ate the book up, which somehow said to me that maybe being poor wasn't the "ending that stopped all beginning" that I thought it was. Not that anything visibly changed, but a little seed of self-respect grew in my chest. When we finished the book Mrs. Hughes dropped the *real* bomb on us—S.E. Hinton was a *woman*! "NO WAY?!," the kids exclaimed. "YES WAY!!," exclaimed my heart. My vicarious seed of self-respect began to explode. This gender revelation turned my world upside down. It was actually *cool* to be a girl. A girl could write a book that made boys crazy to read it and even want to be the characters inside. A girl could write a book that told how it felt to be really, really poor and alone, but made the person reading suddenly feel *not* alone. That's powerful magic for *every* mind. It was a connection crucial to the person I have become. When the kids would call our teacher "Mrs. Huge" after that it made me sad and angry, but I could tell from the message she was sending out about the positivity of books that she was above meanness; books were above meanness. Books were a safe place to be. Therein lies the power of a transformative story!

The love I feel for Mrs. Hughes is echoed here, in the pages of this book, by so many student writers; beautiful postcards from many zip codes to tell these teachers and policy makers "I want to help!" These are honest, inspired responses to the art of great writers like Sherman Alexie and James Baldwin. Statements that seem as simple as "I trust myself when I write," by fourteen-year-old Ulises Mendoza, and sixteen-year-old Julia Peck's "You forced us to speak up and take the question marks out of our mouths" are poetry on the page by themselves, but in this context, together with the other moving student essays, they become a powerful harmony chord of praise and action. The student writers put themselves in the shoes of our leaders, and using intelligence, wit, and compassion they frame solid arguments for the need to keep our teachers happy, our schools open and accessible, and to keep the funding coming in. In the words of thirteen-year-old Yolanda Jordan in her essay about becoming just a statistic ("a dot") when her beloved school closes, she asks: "I wonder now, do you really think, readers, that I am just a dot?" (No way, Yolanda—now I just think you're a bad-ass!)

• • •

Thank you Mrs. Hughes. Thank you brave people—young and old—who write essays, articles, and books; who teach; who make art and take risks. Thank you, especially, you teachers who don't get paid squat for it and still show up *every day.* We need you. Teachers and books—think of the magic they do together for hungry minds and hearts. Love them, respect them, throw them parades, pay them like professional athletes, and set them loose on the world.

—Neko Case

***Neko Case** is a singer/songwriter who won a steadily growing cult audience for her smoky, sophisticated vocals and the downcast beauty of her music. Born in Alexandria, Virginia, Case moved around often as a child, spending the largest part of her youth in Tacoma, Washington. She left her parents at age fifteen, and three years later she started playing drums for several bands around the Pacific Northwest's punk rock scene. Case moved to Vancouver in 1994 to enter art school and simultaneously joined the punk group Maow, which released a record on the Mint label. She also played with roots rockers the Weasles and eventually formed her own backing band, Her Boyfriends, which initially featured alumni of the Softies, Zumpano, and Shadowy Men on a Shadowy Planet. Case's most recent album,* Middle Cyclone *(2009), debuted at number 3 on the* Billboard *charts. The album was nominated for Grammy awards in the categories of Best Recording Package and Best Contemporary Folk Album.*

# 1

# "Thanks for Teaching Me How to Steer": Letters to Educators

In this chapter students wrote letters to teachers who had an impact on their lives. Through these letters we learn how meaningful the relationships between students and effective teachers can be. We also learn how much respect and gratitude students have for their teachers' passions, their kindness, and even their quirks. Most students wrote about teachers who helped them, and a small handful wrote about teachers who failed them. There is so much to learn about the attributes and connections that kids need in their experiences with teachers every day.

# You Interrupted My Dinner

## Julia Peck, age 16
Washington, D.C.

Dear Mr. Hughes,

You started changing my life the night you interrupted my dinner in 2006. It wasn't any fault of yours, actually. My dad had spent the day observing classes at Deal Junior High School, and he set down his fork to make an announcement.

"Today, I saw the best English class I'd probably ever seen in my life," he said. My ears perked up. "He was amazing. He was reading to the class, and he'd fire off questions and they'd be answered immediately. It was interesting, engaging. I really hope you get this guy, Julia. His name's Mr. Hughes."

I pictured you in my head. Great. A drill sergeant. A no-nonsense approach to education, the kind my father would approve of.

But only a few months later, I sat, incredulous and a bit terrified, as you took down a Viking helmet from a shelf and placed it on your head, grinning. It was the first day of school.

"Dilemmas," you announced. You removed the ridiculous hat and held it out in front of you. With your hand between the horns attached to the headpiece, you showed us how a character is caught between two doomed situations: either way they turn, they are figuratively gored by a horn.

Before we'd even opened a book, we could already relate to your message. We'd just been thrust into the terrifying middle school world—where grade populations were suddenly in the three digits, girls whispered insults about third parties into each other's ears, boys struggled to find an acceptable balance between carefree childhood and the pursuit of manliness, freedom hadn't yet come but school was no longer a home, and we strove for attention more than ever but now moved between seven impersonal classes—but suddenly, in your class, things were easy.

We were awkward and self-conscious. You didn't seem to take *yourself* seriously.

We were scared of being wrong. You forced us to speak up and take the question marks out of our voices.

We were used to being closeted and babied. You spoke freely about the facts of life and things we would later face. We read and discussed great literature; before we had maybe been trusted with a Shel Silverstein poem, at most. In Room 215, we were adults, and for that I give you my first thank-you.

But as you guided us to face the coming of adulthood in all of its gritty, stressful glory, you kept the time we spent in your classroom light and unpredictable. In fact, the only thing we knew for certain as we walked into your room each morning was that, at 9:32, one of us would cover an eye and growl, "Arggggh," per your request.

The day could become a discussion of what death does to love as we read "Annabel Lee," or nature versus nurture as we examined why some students excel in school while others struggle. As the year progressed, it became clear to me that you aimed not only to provide us with a solid foundation in literature but also a basic training for life. You understood that at this pivotal time in our lives, we needed to learn English and so much more.

The most glaringly obvious example of your philosophy was our "Seven Habits of Highly Effective Teens" project. Modeled after the genius self-help book of the same title, you asked us to name and give examples of seven attributes of the ideal teenage student, effectively forcing us to lay down the stepping-stones that would support us for years to come. School was suddenly not about learning things important to the teacher's life but about preparing for our own. Thank you.

And reading was no longer just what nerds did when they felt antisocial; to read was to submerge oneself into another world and resurface with new lessons and outlooks on life. You challenged us to find a literary work that didn't have a theme. Tons of stuff, I thought. Disney and comic books and dumb kid stories.

Then you passed out the model book report showcasing the format we'd follow all year. " 'The Three Little Pigs,' by an unknown author, is a story about hard work for a secure future."

I had already concluded you were fairly crazy, so I was tempted not to believe that *The Three Little Pigs* was actually supposed to mean so much. But the more we discussed it, the more mind-blowing it became: authors are telling us much more than a story. I have never forgotten that day, and most likely never will. Thank you.

The rest of the school year went flying by. You laughed at your own jokes, you laughed at us laughing at you laughing at your own jokes. You wore pirate eye patches occasionally; you read poetry with such emotion that I thought you had written it. We deciphered those poems together, all twenty of us. We sang in front of the class, all twenty of us, one at a time, as you had demanded. Sang our *Treasure Island*–inspired ballads to the tune of the *Gilligan's Island* theme song, and when you promised no one would make fun of us, no one did. We traveled through time with *The Glory Field* and *The Devil's Arithmetic* and imagined ourselves in lives so different from our own. It was then that I learned true empathy, as I wrote a journal entry for Chayas, the protagonist of *The Devil's Arithmetic*, as if I were her and realized she wasn't the jerk I thought she was; I would've done the same thing she did.

On the last day of school, you handed out copies of William Ernest Henley's "Invictus." When I got home that day, I propped up the sheet between my desk and the wall, and it wasn't long until I had memorized it. "I am the master of my fate," the last lines read. "I am the captain of my soul." I knew that, Mr. Hughes. But the question was: once you are captain, how do you know where to go? And that's where my final thank-you comes in: thank you for helping teach me how to steer.

Sincerely,

Julia Peck

***Julia Peck** is a high school sophomore in Washington, D.C., and is the daughter of a government employee and a French teacher. She is a debater, runner, soccer player, dancer, journalist, novelist, and human rights advocate with absolutely no idea what she wants to be when she grows (further) up, and she likes it that way. Her addiction to traveling to fascinating places has led her to pursue fluency in two other languages, and she can always be found with a camera around her neck. She devours books like she devours Thai food, and has a penchant for reggae music. After high school and college, she hopes to find herself somehow helping people both at home and overseas and promoting worldwide peace and understanding. She also tends to avoid lofty goals.*

# Like a Chess Game

## Ha Truong, age 18

Washington, D.C.

Dear Mr. Tan,

How have you been? Time has gone by so fast, and I still cannot believe that it has been six years since the last class reunion. I don't think you will be able to recognize me now, as I have grown ultra-huge from the small boy I used to be in your fourth-grade English and math classes.

Those were the best classes I have ever taken, even up until now. I don't think I could have passed fourth grade, especially English class, if it weren't for all the help I received from you. I hope this letter can express fully my thankfulness and respect.

It was not easy for me to walk into your class the first day because, before the fourth grade, I did not know any English words whatsoever. I was actually really nervous because there was no one that I could communicate with because of the language difficulty—or at least I thought so. I actually thought that there was going to be a test at the beginning to see how much we had learned in third grade so that we could be rearranged according to our knowledge.

It is very funny to me now that I got stressed out over silly stuff. When you walked into class, I think the first words you said were "Good morning," but I did not know those words back then. It is incredible how you just took a glance around at all of us and knew that I wasn't able to understand anything, not even the schedule on the board.

I really admired your patience after that day, because I think you had to repeat yourself six or seven times just to get an answer to the question where I was from. I felt relieved to find out later that there was a translator for me in class. It was so great for me that you had a mechanical dictionary; the best memory I have is writing down my questions and you being able to respond. Thank you for letting me borrow it for the first few weeks. It was a lifesaver for me.

It was wonderful that I got to introduce myself a few weeks later, after I learned how from the dictionary. It made me feel much more welcome in class as everybody was cheering and clapping. I think that was the boost I needed to do well in class. And the postcards you forced everybody to draw every day helped out a lot, too. I felt so lucky that I was not a very creative artist because, for every new word I did not know how to draw the meaning immediately (I had a very hard time coming up with ideas), I remembered those words really well by thinking hard about a picture that would represent them. The best part was that you actually hung everybody's work around the classroom, so I think our class was more like a museum than a normal forty-five-student class.

It was not just English class—your math class was amazing, too. I was extremely bad at understanding the questions. I remember how the word "twice" made me fail the first test. I was lucky because you asked me to stay after school for help. I still cannot believe you taught only three of us until 6 PM every day for a whole week. It was the only time I had to do extra work, but I was not tired at all because of the way you made the math equation seem like a game. I remember you said to imagine equations like a chess game, and it was amazing how much easier it became for me. It's too bad that I cannot remember this method now whenever I face a tough problem, but it was so useful that I went from a 58 percent in your class to an 80 percent.

Once again, thank you for everything.

***Ha Truong*** *is a high school senior in Washington, D.C., but was born in Hanoi, Vietnam. His proudest accomplishment is to graduate from high school with a decent GPA. He loves spending time with friends and helping them with their homework, especially with math after school. He will be attending a university next year and intends to do his best, as he's done in high school.*

# Hmmmmm, Yeah, Life Is Good

## Sergio Hernandez, age 17

Ann Arbor

Dear Mr. Long,

This might be unexpected, but it's kind of cool that throughout the four years I've been here, I always knew where I could find you. I could always talk to you about things that no one else would know about. You know, I remember the first time we met. I was a freshman. I didn't know what was going on, and all of a sudden I had to go to an office of some sort. I later found out that it was for a teacher-counseling program. That's when you came up to me and introduced yourself, and that meant you were my counseling teacher.

From there on, I found out you played chess—one of the games I never thought I would play a lot. I had played before, in eighth grade, but I came here, and you taught me many things about the game. You changed a lot of things in my life in a big way, even though this was the first time I'd had you as a teacher. Like showing and opening the doors to this game for me. I learned that in order to go through a normal day, you have to plan what's going to happen, and then most of the time you can control the outcome of your situations. In the game, you have to plan moves through and also make sacrifices; and in my life, I have been in situations where I had to sacrifice things. It also kept me out of trouble. I stayed home and practiced chess by myself instead of being out in the streets, getting in trouble and lying to my mother about where I was.

To this day I still play, and I have learned a lot since I came here. I would play all day, while some people can't stand even hearing the word "chess." But education is the key to success, and this game showed me that it is worth graduating—if I've gotten this far, I might as well finish. Another thing that chess changed over time, as I played and grew up playing, was my mind. I used to be ignorant and did not care about anyone or anything. I used to say to myself, *Man, you don't need this class*, but now I see that I have to pass most of the classes schools give me, whether I like it or not. At the end of the day it's for my own good, and I'll feel better knowing I'm passing.

When I had you as a teacher, I remember you would call my name while we got to work on our own in class. You would talk to me personally about why my grades were so low, and how you could help me raise them. I would tell you that I was trying, and that the grades would improve, and you would give me a funny look meaning that you were not playing any games. Kind of reminded me of my mother when she would get mad at me. You also wanted me to graduate, and, in the nicest way, I could tell you didn't want to see me attend as a senior again. I am glad that we crossed paths and became good friends instead of being just student and teacher. All of this was accomplished with your help, and I am glad that I had someone to count on who showed me that I am not alone.

Thanks to you, I will be the first person in my family to graduate. To me and my family it will be a great honor for me to accept the diploma in front of all of my classmates I've known since I started school. I learned that life isn't simple, and that it's not just going to school every day. There are consequences, like when you make a bad move in chess. One move can cost you the game, and wrong moves with real events can cost you your life. You were a big part of this important realization in my life, and I thank you for that. This comes from the heart. I was on a road walking blindfolded, not knowing what I was doing. But now I can see, and I'm sticking with all my classes. I will fight to fulfill my dreams and make everyone who depends on me proud—most of all, my mother. I'll make her happy when I walk on Graduation Day, and I want her to be proud enough to say, "Yeah, that's my son up there. Hmmmmm, yeah, life is good."

***Sergio Hernandez** is a high school senior in Ann Arbor, Michigan. Though he likes having fun and joking around sometimes, he thinks school is important because it keeps him out of trouble and opens the door for a better future. He loves playing basketball and is a passionate fan and defender of Kobe Bryant. He is known in school for having an extensive collection of Jordans and encourages his peers to refrain from "stepping on his J's." The person he respects more than anyone is his mom, who has always been there for him. He plans to attend Eastern Michigan University.*

# K.I.S.S. the Equation

Sandra Liu, age 17
San Francisco

When I was a third grader, I remember sitting on the bench during recess and thinking about what it would be like if I skipped every single grade and jumped ahead to high school. I was tired of playing kickball with the boys, and I wanted to do what the "big kids" were doing. Now I am a senior in high school, and I find myself wishing school wouldn't end just yet. As I ask myself why I want to stay in school, I think about how I'm going to miss the great teachers who have made an impact on my life throughout these twelve precious years. And for that reason, I want to pay a special tribute to one of the teachers I respect the most, Mr. Kim.

Mr. Kim was my eighth-grade Algebra II teacher. Every afternoon, my classmates and I would line up outside the room, waiting to enter. On some days, we would wait until the last bell rang. Nobody was in the hallway except for us, and all was quiet except for the muffled yelling inside the room. The previous class was a group of seventh-grade math students, and I remember many days when Mr. Kim would keep them inside later than usual. When the doors finally flew open, the students pushed past us with rebellious expressions, grasping little pieces of paper; Mr. Kim was taking his time writing out detention slips. The seventh graders were very rowdy, and their behavior often infuriated Mr. Kim. When we finally marched into his classroom and peered toward the overhead projector for the warm-up assignment we do every day called a "Do Now," we waited silently for the day's lesson and whispered to each other, wondering if he was going to take his anger out on us. However, the thing I admire the most about Mr. Kim was that, despite what had previously happened, he always regained his composure and pulled out the lesson plan for my class.

During the usual days when there was no tension, Mr. Kim stood in the hallway, waiting for us. I would walk into his room chuckling at his latest joke of the day while he greeted students with cheesy high fives. One of his most memorable lesson plans came one afternoon when we were learning the quadratic formula. He told us in his booming voice, "The easiest way to memorize this equation is to say the equation out loud! Everybody together, "Negative b plus or minus the square root of b squared . . ." We watched as Mr. Kim held up his hands as if he were a conductor leading an orchestra. He continued, ". . . minus four A, C over two A," and guided everybody in reciting the quadratic formula until it was drilled into our heads. When it was time to use the formula with math problems, Mr. Kim noticed that I still had some difficulty applying the formula. That was when he told me to "K.I.S.S. the equation." K.I.S.S. stood for "Keep It Simple, Stupid," but in my case, he modified it to "Keep It Simple, Sandra." It was his advice that I should never be intimidated by a problem that looks difficult. He explained that I should be able to do all the problems as long as I kept things simple.

My classmates and I bonded through his activities, and we developed trust in him and each other. Through this trust, the advanced students of the class were able to help the struggling students overcome math fears without anyone feeling superior or inferior. He taught us valuable math skills and gave us a strong foundation so that we would be able to tackle higher-level math courses in the future.

When I graduated from middle school, I found myself holding on to Mr. Kim's advice. Whenever I needed to use the quadratic formula, I vividly remember the day when I first memorized it with

Mr. Kim. I took his K.I.S.S. technique and applied it to other subjects aside from math, and even with life experiences. Mr. Kim was my teacher, my mentor, and my friend, and I thank him for everything I have learned.

***Sandra Liu** was born in 1992 and is a high school senior in San Francisco. She loves to cook and write and is excited to attend UC Berkeley in the fall.*

# Your Smile Said It All

## Heidy Garcia, age 16

Los Angeles

Dear Ms. Castillo,

As an incoming freshman transfer student, I was new to the school, and nobody knew me. I had come from a small charter school, and now I was at a huge public school. I got lost in the crowd and wasn't sure which direction to take. I felt out of place when I didn't have any friends; everyone was in their own little social cliques while I was just an outcast. You helped me feel better in the new environment. Whenever I had questions about anything, I would ask you, and all of a sudden everything would make sense. Something about you was different from the other teachers. I felt your energy every morning in your class. You loved to come to work and teach us. Your smile said it all: it was bright and confident, and it encouraged me to want to be in your class and learn.

The best lesson we did in your class was the *Romeo and Juliet* project. The sixteenth-century language was difficult, but with your silliness and funny jokes, you made it simpler and more understandable. The skits we did in class helped us understand the major concepts of the play. Everyone felt comfortable participating in your activities because you created a safe learning and sharing environment. Even the shy students broke out of their shells. You made class enjoyable when you brought the swords and wigs to class for the acting and fighting scenes. Your teaching style never created a dull day. Everyone liked you; we voted you "Most-Liked Teacher of the Year."

You always kept us laughing with your riddles, jokes, and anecdotes about your past experiences. We were engaged when you taught us because your lessons were fun. I don't know how you did it, but you just did. You had a spirit of goodwill that came across to the class. If anyone was falling behind, you would try to figure out the problem and possible solutions. You weren't aggressive or violent, and you never yelled. You had patience and treated your students as if they were your children. I think that's why many students felt comfortable talking to you and sought advice from you: you were like a mother figure at school.

I felt your concern when you asked me if everything was all right when I returned to school after being absent. Even though nothing serious ever caused my absences, you making sure everything was okay with me made a difference in my school life. It showed me that you cared and that you noticed when I wasn't in your class.

I wished every teacher had your spirit and enthusiasm for coming to class and teaching. You stood at the door and greeted us with handshakes and smiles. Every day I would think it was awkward, but now that I reminisce on your handshakes, I realize that's what made you stand out from all the other teachers: you built a bond with your students.

The biggest and most impactful moment for me was when you told the class you were going to the Philippines to serve for a year in the Peace Corps. This made me realize that you weren't just a teacher, but an actual human being. I remember you had the entire class crying their eyes out. We couldn't believe you were leaving and weren't going to be our teacher anymore. The tears wouldn't stop running. Your decision was out of the blue, and it hit me that my favorite teacher was moving away and I wouldn't see her anymore. You were a one-of-a-kind teacher.

I will never forget you telling me that I can do anything I set my mind to. "You're a smart girl, Heidy," you said. "Work for what you want, and you'll get your rewards. I believe you can become a very successful person in society." Your words made me believe I had the potential to be anything. You gave me confidence to believe in myself.

You were one of the most influential teachers I've ever had. You were truly inspirational and motivational. Your attitude was always positive. You will forever stay in my mind as one of the most distinguished educators I have come across throughout my years in school.

Hugs and kisses and broken fingers,

Heidy

***Heidy Garcia*** *grew up in a tough neighborhood. Joining an all-girl nonprofit college access program called MOSTE (Motivating Our Students Through Experience) helped her avoid the obstacles and bad influences of her surroundings. Heidy's main motivation for doing her absolute best comes from her single, working mother, who has been with her through thick and thin. In the summer of 2009, Heidy was accepted to SECOP (Science Engineering Community Outreach Program) at Loyola Marymount University. Through this summer program, she realized her interest in becoming a civil engineer.*

# My Boy

Jonathan Avila, age 16
Washington, D.C.

He's tall. Built like a hard wall, soft as plaster. His carriage rides strong, but he is gentle without being a coward. My favorite teacher is my longtime friend and mentor Franklin.

He saw me walk through the door of the weight room with my head up high and hands down low. He greeted me with the respect of a man. "No lies, no bull," he said. "Here, we have respect. If you don't show it, then you won't receive it from me!" He said it and it stuck. Every word, every smile, gave me comfort. Franklin is an outreach worker at the Latin American Youth Center in northwest D.C., but his title doesn't describe who he is. He goes beyond that. Franklin is so cool and knows it, but never uses it. He doesn't have to. He's a gentleman but firm at the same time. His personality and the way that he carries himself defines what we call "swag," and from the first moment we met I wanted to learn anything that he could teach me. It made me feel like I had "swag," too.

See, education for me starts with capturing my interest. Franklin captured it naturally. Sometimes school is stuffy and boring, but Franklin is anything but. I laugh my head off when he speaks because he is so happy all the time. Who is happy *all* the time? It's as if his personality has grown since I've known him, too. He has too much to live for to be sad any day of his life. He seems too cool to be sad.

One phrase sums up Franklin: "He's too cool for that." That phrase is inspiring, because it means more to me and those around him every day. He expects us to leave everything on the mat or at the door and better our health, and he molds us to be who we want to be at the end of the day. He went to college for two years and doesn't make that much money, but what he does goes above and beyond. He's still my friend and favorite teacher because he cares. He cared about my well-being as a young child after all I did was procrastinate for six years.

But two months ago I started working out with him. I stopped procrastinating, and it was hard. I was going through a stage in my life where I'd never pushed myself to before, finally taking advantage of what I had in front of me. Franklin's reaction was a smile and a grin that said, "I want you to be healthy!"

The first week I had no treadmill, no weights, just my body to work with. Over time I grew and grew. I had never felt that type of confidence before, and I loved it. Through thick and thin, Franklin gave me self-confidence. After all I did and didn't do, he was there and wouldn't give up on me.

Now I'm too cool to quit school because Franklin has shown me that it's not just about "swag." Education is cool, too.

***Jonathan Avila*** *is a high school freshman in Washington, D.C., and a third-generation El Salvadorian. Jonathan is a participant in many programs at the Latin American Youth Center, including Upward Bound and the Art + Media House. He is very interested in learning about the history of specific cultures, and he was selected to go to the 2010 National Council of La Raza conference in Texas, where he spoke on issues related to youth advocacy. Jonathan will graduate from high school in 2013 and will be the second person in his family to go to college and graduate school.*

# The Self-Taught Student

Sayre Quevedo, age 17
San Francisco

Dear Mrs. M.,

I want to thank you because you said:
"You daydream too often when I'm trying to teach."

I learned
That dreams weave themselves when the mind is idle
And emerge from a chrysalis when the mind is awake.

Because you said:
"You can't read that;
You don't know what those words mean."

I learned
That words are just images, welded into curved black lines.
Learned I could read Hughes's "America" until it sung,
And Dalton's landscapes, sky-blue.

Because you said:
"You talk too often."

I learned

That tongues are to kneading words as lungs are to breathing air
And that every action is a phrase in itself, and every phrase an action.

So thank you,
Thank you for teaching me
To teach myself.

***Sayre Quevedo*** *is a journalist and poet, dabbling in palmistry. His most recent publications include* The Cacophony Anthology, The Poetry of Love Anthology, *and* East Bay Teens Arts and Literature Anthology.

# You Actually Care

## Ruby Buendia, age 18
Chicago

Dear Rauner College Prep Teachers,

I go back and forth just thinking about what happened to me my junior year. What was it that made me change? Who changed me? When did all this start happening? I still can't come up with an answer. All my life I have always taken the easy way out. Every time something got hard, I just quit and moved on. It's a habit that I've developed since elementary school. It's something that I am still trying to overcome.

Hi, it's me, Ruby Buendia. Some teachers have had me, others might not know me. I'm a junior—should be a senior but, yeah, long story. Here's one way to sum it up: I kind of treated junior year as a joke. I came to school, but slept in class or just goofed around. I really didn't care about how I was going to end up. The only thing I could think about was how to get out.

I'm not going to lie: I really wanted to leave. The rules. The work. The discipline. I guess it was just too much for me. At the beginning of second semester, I had made up my mind just to sit there and let time just go by. I watched other kids do their work as I sat there and did nothing but stare. I know I was capable of doing everything that they were doing, and now I don't get why I didn't pick up my pencil and just try.

When I got my transcripts over the summer, I knew I had finally gotten what I wanted: to leave Rauner. When I got what I wanted, it felt like I could breathe, but, at the same time, I felt something was missing. During the summer, I started to think about whether I really had made the right choice, but it wasn't until I started attending my neighborhood school that I saw what this change would really mean.

At my new school students were doing what they wanted, and it seemed that even the teachers were, too. I was so used to the teachers keeping the students on track and motivating us to try our best, but in the new school the only thing they seemed to know was how to give us free periods. As I sat there and watched these teachers "teach," I knew this wasn't for me. I knew I had to come back to Rauner and to you and to do this thing right. It's like they say: you need a fall to pick yourself back up. And every time you pick yourself back up, you keep getting stronger. So I guess what I'm trying to say is that I fell from a very high mountain, and once I fell I got up and just walked away. And once I started walking, I started to see the change. I started to see that everything you guys make us do is for a reason. And all you wanted was to help. When I decided to come back, I knew I had to climb the mountain again.

I guess the point of all this was to tell you I'm very thankful for you guys. You have helped me so much in school. I can still remember the day I was ready to pull my hair out because I didn't understand the word problems in my Advanced Algebra class, so I sat there and just put my head down. Mr. Lessem asked if I needed help, and I said, "No, I just don't *get* it." He told me to stay after school so we could work on it, so I did. When I got impatient he told me to relax, and we just worked through everything step by step. He didn't move for a second while I worked. Students would come in asking for things, and he still didn't move. Mr. Lessem helped them with whatever they needed, but he wouldn't leave my side. I guess he stayed there just in case I had a question. And I liked the fact that he didn't move because it made me realize he really cared. And then, out of the blue, it just hit me. I said, "Oh my God . . . I got it." He smiled and said,

"Let's work through another one." When I left and walked out of his room, I felt so relieved. It felt like I actually did something so good. Since that day, my mind has changed about word problems: I mean, I know they are hard, but I guess what Mr. Lessem taught me was just to break them down.

Every teacher that I've had here always taught in a way that made it interesting. Yes, there were some days that had to be boring, but it was okay because you even warned us that it was going to be boring. So I guess it evened out. You have no idea how much you guys mean to the students. You actually care about our lives and our education. The thing I like the most about the teachers at Rauner is that you guys come to us when you see us struggling. Also, like Mr. Lessem, you guys don't move from your seats until we get it. You try to get the whole class to move through things together, rather than just leave some behind, which could be really easy. I know there are students out there that make it difficult for you guys to teach, but you always find a way to get them back on track. Because you show that you care, students make it easier for you to teach. You've built trust in them.

Mr. Robinson, my literature teacher, was one of the teachers that opened that trust with me. It all happened after the incident with his iPod. In the beginning, I didn't like him. I felt as if he were just picking on me. He would call on me when my head was down. He would tell me to do my work when I was talking. One day, I just got mad and did a kind of childish thing: I stole his iPod. I had that iPod for three whole months, just sitting in my room. I didn't touch it or sell it. It was just always there . . . just staring at me, reminding me that it didn't belong to me. Every day, when I saw Mr. Robinson's face, I was like, "Ruby, you really took his iPod? Man, how *old* are you?" I felt really dumb knowing I did that.

After I stole the iPod, I realized the mistake I had made. I faced the consequences of my actions with a ten-day suspension. When I came back to school, I apologized to Mr. Robinson through a letter. I wanted him to know I wasn't the person he saw in school. I wanted him to know I wasn't a girl who stole his stuff just because she didn't like him. I wanted him to know who I really was. That in reality I am a good person, that I really didn't mean to take it. It just sort of happened. I didn't have anything against him. Honestly, I still don't know what made me steal that iPod. Mr. Robinson wrote back to me and said I was mature and it took courage to admit what I did. Ever since that day, he and I have gotten along really well. Now I can go to him and just talk. Sometimes he even helps me with advice. He is always pushing—I guess because he knows I can do it.

To all of you, I'd like to say thank you once again for everything you guys have done. Your believing in us makes us strive for the best.

Sincerely,

Ruby

***Ruby Buendia** was born in 1992 and is still learning about how life really works. The one thing that keeps her moving is her family—without them, she doesn't know where she would be. Ruby loves to run. It's the thing she does best. Her friends would describe her as funny and trustworthy. Her goal for the future is to accomplish something great from beginning to end.*

# Change for the Better

## Eduardo Diaz, age 13

Chicago

Dear Ms. Reidle,

I just wanted to thank you for helping us when we had problems. Like the time when I got my letter that I had to go to summer school, and I was upset—you made me feel better. You told me that everything would be all right, and to stop being upset, and that I'd learn more in summer school. When my friend lost his grandfather, you took the time to talk with him and make him feel better. This let us know you really cared.

I loved the fun activities we did in science class with you. One of the funniest things I remember is the time you did a flip in the middle of the classroom and your shoe came flying off. It was fun being with you; you always danced, and you were always full of happiness. One time, I remember, we had an assembly and there was music—and out of nowhere you came out and started dancing. By being happy and having fun, you encouraged me to do better in school.

Also, I would like to thank you for spending your free time taking us outside. One day the gym teacher was absent, so our class wasn't going to be able to go outside. You saw us running around thc classroom and knew we had a lot of extra energy. You asked the principal if you could use your free period to take us outside, so that we could run around and play sports and use up some of the energy that we had. Afterward, our class was calmer, and we didn't goof around.

This meant a lot to me because it was another way you showed how much you really cared about everybody in the class.

You helped our class when we had rough problems—not only problems in school, but also problems at home. I would like to thank you for listening to the problems we had. When we had to take the ISAT tests, the whole class was really worried and nervous. But you made us feel better by telling us it was a challenge, like in a video game or on a mission. This made the class feel better about having to take the test.

I wish you were here to see how much I have changed. I have learned more and done a little better at school since you have left. Without your help, I would not have been motivated in school, especially summer school. I'm less shy now, which I like. I've learned how to make new friends and how to pay better attention in class. I played soccer for school last year, as defense. Science is easier for me now than when I was in your class. (Last year, we got to dissect a frog, which was interesting but kind of gross.) Thank you, Ms. Reidle, for always being there. You helped me change for the better.

Sincerely,

Eduardo Diaz

***Eduardo Diaz** was born in 1997, plays soccer, and likes to run. Someday he wants to own a black Mustang, but right now Eduardo enjoys playing with his dog, a boxer named Zoe. He hopes to be a police officer when he grows up. Eduardo likes to goof around and make prank calls to his friends. His favorite food is extra-spicy nachos. He also likes checking out girls—but sorry, ladies, he's taken.*

# I Will Never Forget

## Tatiana Jackson, age 14
Chicago

Dear Mr. Miller,

Thank you so much for pushing me so hard. When older students told me I was lucky to have you as a teacher, I didn't know why—but now I do. You were always very cheery and generous and wore tie-dye all the time. You always tried to be hip, like the time you tried on Ellen's Ugg boots, which we got a big laugh out of. You were very straightforward and didn't mind telling us what was on your mind, even if the truth hurt. You are fun and funny, but also very firm. So it was like you were our friend *and* our teacher. I'm a better person because of it. This has really changed me because you taught me to stay grounded and not drift off with my surroundings. I learned that I didn't always have to hang out with the loud and crazy crowd to fit in. You taught me that I could be really smart and quiet and have just as many friends.

Before your class I always hung out with the cool kids. We got in trouble for hanging out in the seventh-grade hallways, even though we knew that we weren't supposed to be there. We were always pushing and yelling in the hallways. I went along with it because I didn't want the others to think that I was scared, but I hated being in trouble and being labeled.

My turning point was when I got suspended, for the first and only time, for being in the wrong hallway and cursing. When I got home, my mom and I talked about it, and she told me that this wasn't me at all and that if I continued on this path it would only lead to more trouble. She also said that I could be much more if I applied myself. Weirdly, a few days later, you told me the same thing. Then I knew it was time for a change. When I was in school, I analyzed my actions and saw how stupid and immature the things that I did actually were.

At the beginning of the year my grades and attitude were really bad. I got mostly C's and put my friends before school. After I got suspended, I started to focus on school first and then my friends, and I started to hang out with people who had a positive outlook on life. Giving up my old habits was hard, but it paid off. Third quarter I made the B honor roll, and by the fourth quarter, the A honor roll. This was one of the hardest processes that I have encountered so far in my life. But you never gave up on me, and you knew that I could do it.

Now I am a hardworking, open-minded, independent young lady. I might have hated you and your class back then, but now I wish all my teachers were like you and all my classes were like yours. There aren't many teachers who will push their students. But I think we should cherish the teachers who do, because they're usually the ones who have the greatest effect on us.

To you, Mr. Miller, I say thank you. Through thick and thin you taught me the most important thing in life: if I want something in life, I will have to strive and work hard to get it. This is a lesson I will never forget.

Sincerely,

Tatiana Jackson

***Tatiana Jackson*** *loves the color purple and enjoys hanging out with her friends and family. Tatiana would like to be a writer when she* *grows up because she believes it's a great way to express yourself. She's also considering a job working with kids, because they're fun to work with. Tatiana is kind of shy but actually becomes very outspoken once people get to know her. Next year, Tatiana will attend high school in Minnesota, and she looks forward to what she thinks will be a growing and learning experience—one that will get her closer to graduation!*

# Algebra for the Afternoon

Michael R. Thompson, age 15
Chicago

Dear Ms. Novak,

Thank you for clarifying math in a great way and teaching us with understanding. Usually you help our principal with her paperwork and create an impact on the school by working in the office, but one day when Ms. Gonzales was in a meeting, you became our algebra teacher for the afternoon. That day, I absorbed more than I ever had before. When you walked into the room, I knew it would be a good day, because of the way you explained things and because you were always so happy. I'd never had you as a classroom teacher. You came in, calmly told us what you were there to do, and started right away. That day, we were working on formulas for how to use fractions and decimals. We'd been working on these formulas for a while, and I was excited to step up to the challenge. I think that everyone else was excited, too, but I was focused on the problems in front of me.

You stepped up to the overhead projector and explained the problems from the book as you wrote them down, so that we could really see how to figure them out. As you taught, the clear tone of your voice made us alert to what you were asking and see how to solve the problem. You challenged me, and I liked it. You treated us with respect, giving candy to those who had the correct answers, and you made us feel delighted as your excitement rubbed off on us. I felt calm having you teach the class, but also more and more thrilled when you wrote the problems on the board. You were like a math magician. You helped by explaining things clearly with your remarkable voice, circling between our desks to make sure nobody looked at the answers in the back of the book. You probably didn't want to give up your candy for nothing, but more than that I think you wanted to make sure everybody understood the problems so that we could use our knowledge for something bigger beyond just class that day.

Thanks to you, I'm better at fractions and faster at figuring out problems, and this makes me awesome at helping others. My friends Rosendo and Noel sometimes ask me for help, and it makes me feel intelligent and bright.

I would really like to have guidance from you after school because your help affected me more than any math teacher ever has. You helped me understand more and helped me to give my best answer yet on a test question or homework.

Sincerely,

Michael R. Thompson

***Michael R. Thompson*** *looks forward to being a linebacker in high school next year. Someday, he wants to be a professional football player. Michael is not too talkative and not too shy; he's generally a bold and happy person. He likes to joke around with friends and family. He loves pizza for its delicious taste and versatility—you can eat it anywhere! He has been mistaken for both T.I. and Mr. T.*

# Teaching Us About Ourselves

Virginia Urzua Rios, age 18
San Francisco

Dear Aurora Lopez,

Thank you for creating workshops in my class, for just us girls, every week on Thursday through the National Latina Health Organization. Yes, we were in seventh grade, but you taught us important topics such as sex education, teen pregnancy, women's leadership, and Chicano history—topics that can be challenging and problematic among a lot of young women. You broke the silence hiding pieces of my history by revealing hidden facts and arguing with historical texts. You prevented me from becoming ignorant about my own culture.

When you introduced us to the documentary *Chicano!: The Mexican American Civil Rights Movement*, we moved close to the television and began to watch with tears blurring our eyes, making constant shouts and comments as events were narrated. We learned about the Treaty of Guadalupe de Hidalgo and the social movements in the 1960s. Even the term "Chicano" was new to me and my friends in the class. All we knew about our cultural history was that the United States had stolen Mexican land, but we were missing facts, both from our textbooks and from our oral histories. *I did not jump the border; the border jumped me* was a revolutionary phrase, first heard in our community, and we realized that the way we had been treated had terms and labels, that we were all immigrants and minorities.

We looked up to you: your skin matched ours, and your dreams far surpassed what we had allowed ourselves to wish for. You were a Latina, and you were attending college. I don't think at the time I knew anyone in college who had Mexican parents, who considered themselves Mexican American. My friends and I would ask you, "How is college? Is it hard? How are you paying for it?" Your answers were simple for such an accomplishment. We spoke to you in English or Spanish or both, and your response came in the language of our questions.

Remember one of the first sessions? You gave us a timed quiz. We had to put condoms on a banana, and we failed. We were curious, having no practical experience with condoms, so we opened the packages and took the condoms out. Some of us ripped the condom out and some put it on backward; none of us read the instructions. "If you girls were in this situation, you would either be pregnant or have AIDS or HIV, or both. That's why it's your responsibility as a girl to know how this is put on and to have one just in case. What if he does not bring a condom? You'll be like, 'No, honey, I have one right here.' " I guess everyone has sex education, but in this workshop it was different.

Because we lived in a city where many girls are influenced to join gangs, you brought in another documentary about girls in gangs. You broached topics that we might come across in our teenage lives. Who else was going to advise us to overcome the obstacles that our parents and teachers can't give advice about without overreacting? Because you grew up in the same city, you became the second option: we could either follow in a gangster girl's road or yours. We had respect for you because you offered your friendship as a teacher without losing your authority, a quality that most teachers lack.

My best friend, Ivonne, would tell you, "Girl, you have curves like a real Mexican." "Ay, niñas," you would sigh when we would giggle and gossip. I admired your confidence when dealing with topics that many would be too shy or embarrassed to speak of. The connections we all had with you, and the encouragement you provided, made us want to become proud, educated leaders. Your advice was not like any other person's. It came from you, and it had a bigger meaning. Your advice felt more like a responsibility to myself, my family, and my community, rather than a mere suggestion.

Even though your teaching topics were not in the California state standards, by the end of the sessions we were aware of many details often ignored by society. We were very fortunate to learn from you, because no one else was going to have these conversations with us; we would probably have learned them on our own, but only through making mistakes. Since then, I have not come across very many of these topics in school. And yet many of my elders ask why the dropout rate is so high, or why we rebel, join gangs, and generally become ignorant. Maybe it is because these troubled students do not have you to teach them. They will probably never learn about their American history, and how to question what has been told to them. I believe that people of color should have workshops in their schools, to learn their culture and appreciate their origins. Maybe if school districts and state governments supported local nonprofit organizations, then students could benefit from these extra resources. Many schools want diversity among students; we want diversity among the teachers.

What is the purpose of learning math, literature, and science if we don't know anything about ourselves? There is time within the school curriculum for classes like yours to happen. We made it work—we missed one day of physical education a week in order to have time for your class. Thank you for being a role model and like an older sister to us. Your class meant everything to us, because students benefit more from lessons taught by empathetic yet rigorous teachers.

Sincerely,

Virginia Urzua Rios

***Virginia Urzua Rios*** *is waiting for Doctor Who to ask her to be his companion and travel in the TARDIS before she attends UC Berkeley this fall. In the meantime, she will amuse herself by writing in nearly illegible cursive, reading classical literature, and watching movies on the weekends with her family. She was born on the Day of the Innocents (December 28) in Oakland, California. She admires Dave Eggers for opening her mind to pursue a career in writing and hopes to earn a dual science and writing degree.*

# What If?

Jessica Volodarsky, age 17
San Francisco

Dear Ms. Koivisto,

How dare you instill the knowledge of chemistry into my mind? Teachers are supposed to mold students' supple minds, not resculpt them. I was once optimistic and carefree. Wandering aimlessly and making choices on a whim, I never had to ask "What if?" It's true I did not always understand what dioxins or GMOs were, know that I could get cancer from my lipstick, or see how I could be a catalyst for the changes in the environment. But naïveté was a part of my charm. Now that I can hear your ever-reverberating voice from miles away, I have become acutely aware of the disintegration of the environment, and, more importantly, that I actually have to do something about it. I am forced to overthink and rethink every seemingly frivolous choice I make because it will all affect my future. Do you know the kind of pressure I am under? You have turned me into a cynic, a glass-half-empty kind of observer. I look at a Safeway grocery bag and cringe, thinking about how it will either end up in a dolphin's stomach or on the floating island of plastic twice the size of Texas in the Pacific Ocean. I have probably spent a week's allowance on reusable canteens, all of which I have either lost or broken. Ignorance made me content until the gloom of knowledge cast a paralyzing shadow of foreboding on Earth's impending apocalypse.

You have changed my outlook on the environment and unwittingly turned me into a closet pessimist. In high school, students are drilled to learn the basics, to meet requirements, and, hopefully, to graduate. Leaving school with even a grain of usable knowledge, particularly in chemistry, can be a rarity. Students often graduate blind to how chemistry works in the environment and the suffering that our current planet is enduring. Even though I can balance a redox reaction, form titrations, and calculate molarity, these tools pale in comparison to the exponentially more useful and vital lessons you taught me throughout my year in chemistry—lessons that branch out from the orthodox confinement of public education and graduation requirements. I was warned that chemistry would be the root of all my sophomore misery. I even considered dropping it before the fall semester started. Maybe I should have, because then I would not be so angry; I would not be so terrified wondering when everything will collapse and my children's children's children will die from smog poisoning or acid rain. You are the cause of both my cynicism and my awareness of the environment, and because of you I will always wonder, "What if we continue to neglect the earth—what will happen to the planet?"

Sincerely,

Jessica Volodarsky

***Jessica Volodarsky*** *is a visual arts student who spends her days painting, drawing, and doodling. Jessica hopes that her passion for art will take her to the East Coast after she graduates from high school.*

# You Are One of Those Teachers

Carrie Hutcheson, age 17
Washington, D.C.

Dear Mr. O'Steen,

It is an unfortunate fact of life that great teachers—teachers who inspire their students, teachers who love what they do and are good at it—are rare. You, however, are one of those teachers.

I did not know what it meant to have a truly great teacher until I started taking your Physics I class this year. As someone who has always struggled in math and science classes, I was not looking forward to learning physics, and I began the class with the attitude that I just had to pass and get it over with. You have had a huge, positive impact on the way I view physics to such an extent that I sometimes imagine myself as a high school physics teacher. I have gone from dreading every class and constantly fearing that I would fall behind to looking forward to tackling the next lesson. No matter what I end up doing in life, I know that I will not stop until I find something that I am as passionate about as you are about teaching, and I have you to thank.

You are more than a good teacher; you are a good person. You are always kind and considerate, and I appreciate how you always personally greet me and say good-bye to me whenever you see me. It makes me feel like a person, not just a student the administration is trying to control. A lot of teachers talk down to me or boss me around unnecessarily, but you have never done that. By collecting our notebooks to check that the class has been taking notes and doing the labs, and then writing little notes back, you make me feel acknowledged. They are not always comments on the work I have done; they are sometimes funny remarks, like the time you wrote "Saweet!" in response to my revealing that you were my favorite teacher this year. It might have been a little embarrassing for you, but it was highly amusing for me.

Mr. O'Steen, you never assign busywork, so I never feel as if we wasted any time in class. You really give your students the best of both worlds, because you also never assign tedious work or overload us. You are always fair in the amount of work you assign, the difficulty of the work, and the way that you grade it. Everything we have done this year has been creative and engaging, especially the egg-drop project. Everyone really got into designing their egg-carrying vessels, using only ten pieces of paper, a limited amount of tape, and four plastic straws. We got to apply principles of physics in an unorthodox way, building our egg-holders and then dropping them from various heights to see whose vessel was the most effective in keeping the egg from breaking.

I have never enjoyed working hard as much as I do in your class. At the end of every class I feel as if we have accomplished an impressive amount of work, but I never feel burnt out or frustrated. I appreciate the effort you put in every day. Besides having a set lesson plan each day, you make yourself available before and after school and during lunch to help students complete pending assignments and make up missed work.

You do not simply assign work and leave it up to us to get through the class. You sincerely care how well each individual student does in the course. I want to do well not only for myself but also for you. I am succeeding in physics because I decided to put in as much effort as you do, and because I respect you and want you to respect me, too.

Above all, the quality that made me realize how wonderful a teacher you are is your excitement. Sometimes, after you finish solving a complex problem or give a long speech about a lesson, you sigh and say, "Man, that's cool," or something like that. Usually, the entire class laughs, but I have to admit that your enthusiasm is infectious. I will never forget the time that you ended a long spiel tying together concepts we had learned with the phrase ". . . and that is the beautiful flower that is physics."

I have been in the District of Columbia public school (DCPS) system since I began my education, and it pains me to say that I did not have an excellent teacher after elementary school until I began taking physics. I am sure that you will have a lasting effect on my life, because, just by your example, you taught me to work tirelessly until I find something that I will be happy doing for the rest of my life. Thank you so much for everything you have done for me.

Sincerely,

Carrie Hutcheson

***Carrie Hutcheson*** *was born and raised in Washington, D.C., although she now resides in Ann Arbor and is attending the University of Michigan. She is majoring in English and hopes eventually to find a position at the* Washington Post.

# Mixing It Up a Bit

Claire Gillooly Dempsey, age 15
Washington, D.C.

Dear Ms. Ma,

As you may know, looking forward to a class is a very unusual thing to see in a normal high school student. But once in a while, you find one of those teachers who, no matter what, will mix it up a bit. I stumbled upon one of such educators two-and-a-half years ago when I entered the eighth grade. I had surpassed the levels of French education available in my middle school, and I was ready for a new linguistic challenge: Chinese, why not? Even on the first day I could tell how excited you were to be sharing something so close to your heart, something you'd grown up with. China and everything about its culture were very important to you, and you made that clear very quickly. You thought of yourself as a representative of your country. Not only did this add to your motivation, but it also made you want to teach us about every aspect of China that you possibly could.

You used many teaching techniques, such as creative games, songs, dances, and even cooking. You always wanted our input on things and were interested in our lives. You gave us every opportunity you had to invite us to participate in something. There were many times where we were invited to perform a song and dance. Once you asked us to cook a Chinese dish to bring to class and to create a poster explaining the process and displaying pictures. Another time, you just decided that we would make dumplings! Ms. Ma, you were always coming up with new ideas and surprising us, always trying your best to make it work. Your efforts always motivated us to try our best.

There were definitely many things you said that I will never forget. You were still learning English when you came, so you would make small mistakes that we would find rather amusing. For example, a fellow student once said she knew the answer but didn't feel like raising her hand, and you replied, "Oh, Jia, you sooo spicy!" To this day, none of us students know what you really meant by "spicy," but nonetheless it is something quirky that we will all remember.

Although you were my teacher you were also sort of a friend. You were always making the effort to try and get to know each and every one of your students. There was no one who didn't like Ma Lao Shi and who didn't have an individual bond with you. Sometimes, my friends and I would even have Chinese tea parties with you on the weekends.

Your love and appreciation of China always shone through. For instance, during the summer of 2008 when Beijing was hosting the Olympics, you were overjoyed and created many activities related to the exciting event. You also showed us movies that you thought could teach us something about the culture and history of your beloved China. You even incorporated kung fu into your lesson plan from time to time. Whatever would spark our interest, you would give it a shot.

Whatever the subject may be, having a teacher who genuinely cares and knows about what they're teaching gives students more motivation. To see your excitement would make us not want to let you down. I hope you know how you have made an impact on each and every one of our lives. In the beginning, when people would say that we were going to be the future leaders of the world, I didn't believe them. But as you have introduced us to so many auspicious programs, I am starting to believe that learning Chinese really does make us more likely to make a difference.

Without you, I don't think I would have the enthusiasm for a foreign country like I do about China. Although I still take French, my teachers have not displayed a passion for the French culture like you do for China's. Even though I still haven't been there, I hope to visit soon!

So I just wanted to say thank you for opening our eyes to so much culture. I hope you continue to spread enthusiasm like you did with us. I don't know if you realize the extent of your efforts, but we sure will never forget them! Thanks for always being there as an educator, and as a friend (as cheesy as that sounds). You always made things fun, yet you still kept your priorities. I hope you learned a lot in the United States and enjoyed your time here, and I plan on continuing to learn Chinese for as long as possible.

Your former student,

Claire Gillooly Dempsey

***Claire Gillooly Dempsey*** *is a high school sophomore. In her spare time, she runs track and spends time with friends. She is intrigued by foreign languages, such as Chinese and French, and hopes to attend school abroad. In the future, she would like to learn more languages and teach English in a foreign country. She wishes she had a talent for cooking.*

# In My Memories and Calculator

Christopher Goodwin Jones, age 16
Washington, D.C.

Dear Mrs. English,

In every successful student's life, there are many elements that strongly impact him or her. Many have access to life-altering literature, strong-willed parents, and, most of all, a group of wise and unique teachers. In this group there is always one teacher that sticks out for a pupil. Whatever aspect of the teacher it may be, whether he or she is strict or free-willed, the connection is there. Every student can identify with this feeling: to be watched over, to be encouraged, to truly and eagerly learn. When I walked into John Eaton Elementary School for my first day of fourth grade, you stuck out.

My memory of fourth grade is marked with many of your sayings and lessons. Although you said time and time again that I was "one who flew over the cuckoo's nest" and that I had the "gift of gab," you stayed by me and heightened my knowledge and love of my favorite subject, math. You challenged me to solve sixty equations in sixty seconds over and over again until I mastered it. Making sure I never had a chance to breathe easy, you instituted an advanced class for me to keep pressing forward in my mathematic campaign. Whenever I need to use the Pythagorean theorem, I think back to the day when I first learned it from you.

Even after I left your class, you still watched over me. I love your letters and cards asking me how I am doing and if I need any help.

It makes me feel truly supported, and I thank you for that. When I heard of your retirement, I thought of all the unlucky students who wouldn't be able to benefit from your great teaching. I am sure many of them would have bonded with you easily, just as I did when I was their age.

Although I must say good-bye again, I hope you know that you are always with me, in my memories and by my calculator. You are my favorite teacher of all time, and I estimate you will remain so for years and years to come. Unless someone cooler comes along. (I'm just kidding.) I'm still "one who flew over the cuckoo's nest" and I think I still have "the gift of gab." You didn't seem to have a problem with it, but I think some other teachers do. I miss you.

Sincerely,

Christopher Jones

***Christopher Goodwin Jones,*** *or C.G. Jones as some call him, is a rising high school junior. Born and raised in Washington, D.C., Christopher feels a true connection with his city. He is often serving his community through planting, cleaning, and spending time with the elderly. Through writing poetry and the occasional short story—all inspired by his city, of course—C.G. Jones hopes to provide a clear face and representation of what it's like to live in Washington.*

# Dear Chemistry Teacher

Jasmine Franco, age 18
Ann Arbor

I always sat in the back of your class, listening to what you had to say. But you never included me. When I wanted to be included, you never listened. Since the first day of class, I knew we weren't going to get along. I walked in the door, and your tone was upsetting and unpleasant. Just the way you acted in class made me uncomfortable. I felt left out when you favored the kids who grasped the information right away, but you seemed upset with the kids like me who had a difficult time. I never had your full attention when I requested it. Everything else seemed more important to you than the question I had to ask.

It has gotten to the point where I don't want to show up to your class anymore because it is so frustrating. I cannot have a real conversation with you because you don't listen. You are so close-minded that all you do is raise your voice, say what you want to say, and walk away.

I cannot forget the time you made me cry in front of the whole class. It was the worst moment I have experienced in school. You made me cry, and the whole class heard me. I had a late pass to get to class. I was excused, but when I knocked on the door, you came out and told me to call my parents and then you shut the door in my face, leaving me outside the class. Now I faced the hardest part, because I did not have anyone to call. I had no parents in the United States.

But how would you know that if you never took the time to know the lives of your students?

During my junior year, my parents got deported to Guatemala. Everything happened so suddenly that I did not get a chance to realize I was going to be on my own, that I wasn't going to be with my parents anymore. I stayed by myself in our trailer; I worked in the evenings as a supervisor in a building to support myself. I got out of work very late, and by the time I came home I was exhausted. It was hard to get my homework done at night and be ready in the morning for school. Even if we are not considered adults, some of us have to be ones anyway. Teachers should listen to their students. You would see that we too have problems as big as adults'.

Your tone really upsets me—the thing you do best is yell at us. Many students don't care. They just take it as a joke, but I don't. I do care. Not even my mother, who has more right than you to do it, yells at me like that. I cannot learn this way. I would learn better if you were nice to me and acted as though you care about your students.

High school was very difficult. I had no parents to pay the bills like any normal teenager did. Working made it really difficult, because I got home around 11 to 11:30 P.M. and I did not have time to do my homework. I was so surprised when I got the letter saying that I had passed eleventh grade. Then, having to face a teacher who was not nice and not willing to help only made things worse. I even thought about dropping out of school, but decided it was the wrong way to go. I want to inspire my family and anyone else who is around me.

I am not writing this letter to let you know how bad you are. In fact, I am writing to tell you that you are a really knowledgeable teacher. You know so much: I just wish you would care if I learned it or not. I want to take advantage of your knowledge, but I cannot do that if you don't let me. I came to learn about chemistry, but I will have to teach you another kind of chemistry, one that you don't know: how to bond with your students, to have fun, and to make learning more interesting.

***Jasmine Franco** is a high school senior in Ann Arbor, Michigan. She was born in Chicago, but her parents are from Guatemala. She works for Washtenaw County Workers Center as a community organizer and teaches ESL classes for adults at her church. Her proudest accomplishment is that she is graduating from high school this summer, the first in her family to do so. She enjoys translating and helping people in her community and is a natural-born cook. She plans to go to college to pursue a career as a nurse practitioner.*

# A Raffle Ticket Kind of Teacher

Natali Salcedo, age 15
Washington, D.C.

Dear Ms. Meagher,

I would just like to thank you for being a phenomenal teacher throughout fifth grade. Even when you were trying to help the other twenty-three students in the room, I felt as if I was your top priority. Every time I needed help, you were there. You helped me push through the difficult times I had with fractions, spelling errors, and much more.

You never ceased to amaze me with how you could keep us entertained and teach the required material at the same time. I think that the assignments you gave us were part of the reason why we flourished. Remember when you assigned us our class project in which we had to take photos of our shoes and explain how each style meant something different to us? Well, that was probably one of my favorite assignments. It was creative, fun, and original. It took me three hours to finally finish, but I ended up having a really good time while working on it. Another one of the assignments that I really enjoyed doing was researching a topic of my choice and then making a pamphlet on it. I thought this was something good to assign because when you get to pick what you want to work on, it makes the work more interesting and a lot easier. For me, it was easier to make the pamphlet because I had prior knowledge about the topic.

After making the pamphlet, we set up stations in which people could share their information with others.

Not only did you give good assignments, but you also had a great attitude toward learning. You seemed very passionate about teaching. If a student did not understand what you were teaching, you would try your best to help them out. You had several methods that you used to try to help kids that needed it, but the thing you were best at was staying calm. Too many teachers tended to lose their cool with their students when they didn't understand, or because they simply didn't have enough patience, but with you it was different. You understood that if someone didn't get what they were taught at first, that didn't mean they wouldn't eventually get it. You stayed with your class until you were sure that all your students understood everything.

In addition to being a dedicated teacher, you had a funny personality. Although some of your jokes were a little cheesy, it was fine because everyone had a good time listening to them. I remember hearing a snort every time you laughed, which made it even funnier. I enjoyed being in your class for many reasons, one of them being that we didn't get an excessive amount of homework—instead, you emphasized learning the material in class. My fifth-grade year was definitely one of the years in which I learned the most in elementary school.

We had many fun times together in class throughout the year. The most fun experience we shared together was not during school, however. I won a raffle ticket to see a movie with you and a friend. I invited my best friend at the time, Chloe, to come with us. We had a blast making fun of you because you had expired jam, coffee cups, and mustard packets scattered inside your car. But that wasn't the only reason why we had fun. It was also nice just to be talking with you and a friend in an environment that didn't involve chaos. I think it was that night when I realized that you were my favorite teacher.

I will never forget the moment when you told me that if I ever needed help or anything from anyone, I should come see you. So far in my life, I have not exactly needed much from others, but I know that if I ever do, you'll be one of the first people that I would go to. This is not just because you told me this, but also because I trust you, and I know you would guide me through whatever problem I needed help with. You were one of the few teachers I could automatically trust with anything.

Well, what I am trying to say to you, Ms. Meagher, is that you were, and probably still are, an amazing teacher. Not only because of the things you did in class, but also because I knew you outside class. You had a large impact on my life. I hope you continue teaching and spreading knowledge to your upcoming students. Good luck with everything that is to come, and I hope to see you soon.

Sincerely,

Natali Salcedo (one of your favorite students)

***Natali Salcedo** is a sophomore in high school in Washington, D.C. She was born in D.C. and has lived there all her life. Her parents are from Columbia and Michigan. She is bilingual in English and Spanish. In her free time Natali enjoys hanging out with her friends and family. She also enjoys playing soccer for her travel team. She hopes to continue to play soccer at a higher level in college.*

# If It Weren't for You

Ryan Hotchkiss, age 17
Ann Arbor

Dear Ms. Edwards,

I remember back in elementary school, when I was new to Pittsfield Elementary School and starting third grade. My family and I had just moved from Cincinnati, Ohio, to Ann Arbor, Michigan. I thought I would have the same problems I had had back in Ohio at my elementary school. My first-grade teacher would not help me with my schoolwork even though it was obvious I needed help. I took a standardized test in second grade, and the results indicated that I had dyslexia. The only people willing to give me the attention I deserved before the test were my parents.

I thought that, with my disability, I would stand out and be made fun of. I was also scared because there was the chance I would have another teacher like my first-grade teacher, who ignored me and left me to fail. The miserable experience of first grade made me really dislike school. But you made me feel welcome, and I was able to open up to you. You made me realize that school is not the worst thing in the world. You found ways to make learning exciting by keeping school interesting.

When I was slipping in classes, mostly during third grade, you and my parents were the only ones willing to help me. I was quite far behind in reading and spelling. There were days when I did not feel like learning anything because it was too challenging. But you were always there, motivating me to do my best and helping me divide the work into smaller tasks to make it easier. You convinced me to break it down word by word and to take my time. Even when things got tough, you still stayed with me and never gave up. You helped me work through all of my problems.

You truly helped me take my reading to the next level. I remember you spending countless hours helping me stick with it by staying with me every step of the way. If it hadn't been for you, I would not have been reading at a fifth-grade level in fifth grade. I thought it would be impossible after barely reading at a first-grade level in third grade. You took the time to work with me in a small group, and forced me to do what I didn't want to do but what needed to be done: read, read, and read.

I appreciate that, after teaching me in elementary school, you began tutoring me once a week at your house. I feel like seeing you every week helps me stay on track at my current level, and even improve. There is nothing that I can say or do to show how much I appreciate you for what you have done to help me be successful in school.

Dyslexia made it really challenging for me to read and write; you helped me push through to succeed. At first I thought school was pointless, but you helped me understand that being successful in school will help me become successful in life. The ACT is coming up, and I am eternally grateful for all your help and the time you have put into making sure I perform at the best of my ability. I will use all the tips you have given me, and I will be even more prepared for the ACT than for the PLAN test I took last year.

If it weren't for you, I would not be where I am today. You gave me the push needed to get my head straight and to work hard in school. Thank you. Thank you for everything. Thank you so much, from the bottom of my heart.

I look forward to seeing you every Sunday, and I will miss you when I go to college. Thanks again, and I hope that some day I can do for you what you have done for me.

Sincerely,

Ryan Hotchkiss

***Ryan Hotchkiss*** *was born in Milford, Ohio, in 1992. He moved to Ann Arbor, Michigan, in 2000. He manages his high school basketball and volleyball team. He also plays volleyball for a recreation league through the fall, winter, and spring, and spends the summer playing basketball. He wrote this letter because he wants to inspire others who may be struggling with a similar disability. With hard work and determination, nothing can hold a person back from reaching goals in school and in life.*

# They Matter, As Long As You Make Them Matter

ChyAnne McKinney-Thomas, age 18
Ann Arbor

Dear Ms. Why,

Before I was even accepted into your already overcrowded African American literature class my junior year, I had heard so many great things about the class and your teaching skills. So I went into the class with high expectations. I came ready to learn, and I did. When I walked in, I thought to myself, *These kids are bad, and how is this little ol' white lady gonna teach us about African American history and literature?* But as soon as you began, everyone stopped talking. The tone in your voice let everyone know that it was time for business. You could even feel the mood change, as if everyone were in the spotlight. If anyone was still whispering, the people around them yelled at them and they stopped talking. The students in this class took it seriously, and at the beginning I could not figure out why. But in time I found out.

You took simple, everyday, basic things, and made them complex. You made us look at things in a totally different way. You made us look as both an outsider and an insider. You took our minds and handed them back to us and made us think for ourselves. You helped us use the voices we had always had but had been too afraid to use. You gave us a chance to be ourselves, the smart young adults that we are. You taught us all about covert, overt, internalized, and institutional racism. You took movies like *Do the Right Thing*, *Bamboozled*, and *American History X* and dissected them. You made us watch each movie, like, three times. Once on our own and two more times with you, breaking things down—sometimes word for word. I watch movies in a totally different way now. I catch the important things and not just the jokes. I closely watch what people say and pay attention to how they say it. In Ms. Why's class, no one is shy. No one is afraid. Everyone's thoughts and opinions matter. They matter, as long as you make them matter.

I just want to thank you. You really made a great impression on my life. You helped me see and think about things that have always been there, but I was just too afraid to actually take it that far. You were the first (and hopefully the last) teacher I've cried in front of. You stayed after class, after school, and helped me do whatever I needed to do. You pushed me to handle my problems on my own and made me take a look at myself and what I was doing wrong. You made me work for myself, which I am used to, but there was just something different about doing it in school.

I could go on and on, but I won't. I just wanted to thank you for your time and patience. You really care about your students and where they end up in life. It's very hard to find teachers like that.

Thank you.

***ChyAnne McKinney-Thomas*** *is a high school senior in Ann Arbor, Michigan. She works at a local McDonald's in her neighborhood. She likes to sing but is also very interested in law. She's even thinking of becoming an investigator if music doesn't work out. She's a very down-to-earth person. Sometimes she feels very misunderstood; most people think she is mean when they first meet her, but really she is a loving, caring, and sensitive person with a huge heart. She loves laughing and believes it's good for the soul. She stays close to her small but loving circle of friends and to her mother and grandmother.*

# Building Confidence

## Ulises Mendoza, age 14

Chicago

Dear Ms. Dunn,

I'd like to thank you for helping me and encouraging me when I needed it the most, especially when we were studying the Constitution. If we didn't pass the Constitution test, we were not going to be able to go to eighth grade. I was really nervous about this because at first I had Ds and Fs on the practice test, but, by the time the actual test came, I got a 100 percent. You always gave me encouragement by telling me that I was a good student and I was smart, so why would I want to stay in seventh grade? Because of this I studied every day. I started doing flash cards, and kept reading until I got the civil rights movement and the Constitution fixed in my memory. I started getting soccer out of my mind for a while, because it was for my own good not to go to summer school. No one likes to go to summer school.

Not all teachers are as encouraging as you, and you gave me a lot of attention. It meant a lot to me because, since sixth grade, you have been telling me that I am a great student. I think that all teachers should be like you because you always encourage people to do their best. When students don't understand something, you always go over and explain it to them. I remember when I was studying for a test and you helped me with flash cards, which helped me learn the questions and answers much faster. I passed the test with a great score.

Ms. Dunn, I think that some things I have in common with you are that we both like to be healthy and play sports. We also like to be with our friends and talk to people we know and share things that have happened to us. Sometimes I share things that happened with my family, and I enjoy expressing myself to people. When I'm talking, I enjoy that other people are hearing my story. I can tell you are the same way, the way you talk about things that happen to you, when you go to different places, or the day you met Barack Obama when your sister graduated from college. You like to express yourself and not keep anything inside of you. I think this self-expression is important because, if you keep it inside, you might feel uncomfortable. It's better to share with your family and friends. I learned some of this from having you as a teacher, and now I have more confidence in myself and don't pay too much attention to what other people say.

When I go to high school next year, I'm going to take with me the ability to be around a lot of people and communicate with them and be close with my friends. This is going to help me with my grades and with talking to people. Before I met you, I was a shy person who didn't want to talk to anybody, just a person who wanted to keep everything to himself. When I was like this, I wanted to be alone and have my privacy. When I met you, I started talking to more people and getting with my friends. You encouraged me to do this by writing my thoughts down before I spoke to someone; this let me express my feelings better before I had to do it out loud. It took me two months to learn not to be shy in front of a lot of people, but you used to tell me not to be afraid to talk in front of a crowd. When I started talking to other people, I realized it's better to talk to someone than to be alone.

The things you have taught me have helped in soccer, too. I used to get nervous playing because a lot of people were watching me, but your advice helped me to relax. You told me to play the way I usually do. That affected me a lot. I used to not focus on the game and be scared, and I wasn't able to play the way I usually played when I was just with my friends. Now I play better, and next year I plan to get into school sports; that way I can hopefully get an athletic scholarship. I want to play soccer professionally when I grow up. That's a dream that my brother and I both want to follow. My brother was a great player. He heard from a really important soccer company and was going to do well, but then he got hurt and can't really play anymore. I want to realize his dream and my dream by becoming a soccer player.

If all teachers were like you, Ms. Dunn, then all students would have the same opportunities as I did to succeed. You helped me with myself and in my life. You helped me gain confidence in myself and to be proud of what I do. This makes me feel really good.

Sincerely,

Ulises Mendoza

***Ulises Mendoza*** *was born in 1996, enjoys drawing, but he says mostly he "likes to write, and I trust myself when I'm writing. I like to be around people who talk about their problems, and to help them." Ulises also likes going to parties and would describe himself as a bit of a party animal. He enjoys dancing, but most of all he enjoys playing soccer. Ulises can be found playing middle-to-right (unlike his brother Ivan, who plays up front). Ulises prefers Eminem to M&Ms, and would even go so far as to say he does not like chocolate. To keep himself in shape, Ulises does not eat much candy at all.*

# My Very Best Teacher

Ashley Jones, age 17
Washington, D.C.

Dear Ms. Jones,

I wanted to let you know that you were my very best teacher. You made the third grade one of the best times of my life. Learning in your class was phenomenal—you made education fun. You always incorporated fun activities with educational learning. I loved how you taught us multiplication; playing "Around the World" was the best. Sitting in a circle with someone behind you racing to answer the multiplication question correctly first was extremely fun! It kept us interested and always anxious to play the game. I remember that on days we did not behave in class, you did not let us play "Around the World." We were crushed, but it was for the right reasons.

I know it sounds like I'm repeating myself, but I really enjoyed your class. Even though third grade was so long ago, I loved coming to your class because you were very enthusiastic and enjoyed teaching my class. I loved how you always praised us for doing good things by taking us out on Saturdays, doing fun extracurricular activities. I remember when I completed all my homework and received all the stars on the homework chart, you picked me up and took me, Claudia, and Ana to go mini-golfing and to see the movie *CatDog*. That day is so memorable to me not just because you were my teacher, but because you always went the extra mile to make us happy.

I have so many memories of that third-grade class. My most memorable moment is the day when you took us to visit your alma mater, American University. You had us third-graders thinking and dreaming about college at such an early age! I love how we ran American University's track, and because you are a former track star you came in first place. I also remember one of our very best class assignments, when you read us *The Little Engine That Could* and told us we could never say, "I can't" because the little engine always said, "I think I can, I think I can." You instilled the belief not only in me but in the rest of the class that we *can* do whatever we put our minds to.

I loved and to this day still remember the class assignment you did with magnets. No matter how hard we pushed the two magnets together, they never touched. As a class we were amazed but frustrated by the results, but you explained that it's a part of science and its forces.

Ms. Jones, it's been nine years since I've last seen you, and I wonder where you are and if you love other children like you loved my third-grade class. I'll never forget the educational games you played with us. I definitely will never forget how I learned my multiplication tables by playing "Around the World" and all the other fun lessons. I will never forget the day you took me mini-golfing and out to see *CatDog*. I will never forget how you were available day or night; the class could always reach you if we needed you. I will never forget how bummed the class would be when it was time to go home and we had to copy the homework from the board. We loved copying your signature at the bottom of the board because you would put smiley faces inside your "J."

Ms. Jones, I'll never forget you, and one day I hope to see you again. I just wanted to let you know that, because of you starting me off thinking and dreaming of college, this is the year that I finally get to go! It is because of you that I am majoring in elementary education so that one day I'll become a third-grade teacher. I want to instill what you've taught me to kids in the third grade. Ms. Jones, you are my inspiration. I love you.

Sincerely,

Ashley Jones

***Ashley Jones** is a high school senior in Washington, D.C., and has lived there her entire life. She loves children and aspires to become a third-grade teacher for Durham North Carolina Public Schools. She wants to work in Durham because she is attending North Carolina Central University. She is a double major, studying elementary education and social work. She hopes to get her master's degree and inspire many third-graders along the way.*

# 2

# "Bobbing When I Should Have Weaved": Vignettes Inspired by Sherman Alexie

In this chapter students from all over the country were inspired by Sherman Alexie's piece called "Indian Education" where he shares his school experience through a series of short essays. Young 826 writers then created stories about themselves using Mr. Alexie's technique. After they wrote their pieces, he read their pieces and wrote a response to them.

Enjoy! Maybe you'll be inspired to share your stories, too. We hope so.

# An Introduction

In 1989, when I was twenty-three years old and an aspiring poet at Washington State University, I had to borrow my then-girlfriend's electric typewriter to write. While I certainly love my computer and high-speed Internet, I fondly recall the primitive grace of that old typewriter (I wonder if my ex-girlfriend still owns it; I'd certainly buy it from her). For those of you who might not remember typewriters, you had to thread in one sheet of paper at a time. And once you filled up that sheet, you pulled it out and threaded in another and another and another until you'd finished your essay or term paper. However, when it came to poetry, I discovered that I could not write a poem longer than one sheet of paper. The physical act of pulling out that one sheet always made me stop writing. It was a strange tic.

So, when I took my first fiction writing class, I knew I'd have to write more than one page. But how was I supposed to do that? How could I overcome my one-sheet addiction? Well, I decided to fool myself. I decided to write a story broken down into one-sheet segments. But what would those segments be?

I have always been a very autobiographical writer, so I decided that a year-by-year accounting of my elementary and secondary education might be cool. So I wrote fictionalized versions of the major events—and minor events that felt major—of each of those years, titled it "Indian Education," and turned it in.

My teacher loved it. My classmates loved it. I was surprised by their affections. I just thought the story was a simple exercise, a warm-up for something more complex and larger—a story that would stand the test of time.

Well, twenty-one years later, my simple story still resonates with people. I am always amazed and flattered by anybody who wants to read my work, but to think that a story can still retain power for people two decades after its creation seems like a miracle.

And so these stories by the young writers from the 826 chapters feel like miracles, too. I love the energy and the humor, and the sadness and pain. I love how my story, broken into segments that simply enabled me to write past one page, lends the same sort of energy to these young writers.

But I most especially love how the story of a reservation Indian boy can resonate with the urban kids of our country, and how the stories of those urban kids resonate with the Indian man I have become.

Dear readers, I think you'll recognize yourself in these stories. That's a great thing.

—Sherman Alexie

Here is the piece the students responded to:

## Indian Education

(from *The Lone Ranger and Tonto Fistfight in Heaven* by Sherman Alexie)

### FIRST GRADE

1. My hair was too short and my U.S. Government glasses were horn-rimmed, ugly, and all that first winter in school, the other

Indian boys chased me from one corner of the playground to the other. They pushed me down, buried me in the snow until I couldn't breathe, thought I'd never breathe again.

2. They stole my glasses and threw them over my head, around my outstretched hands, just beyond my reach, until someone tripped me and sent me falling again, facedown in the snow.
3. I was always falling down; my Indian name was Junior Falls Down. Sometimes it was Bloody Nose or Steal-His-Lunch. Once, it was Cries-Like-a-White-Boy, even though none of us had seen a white boy cry.
4. Then it was a Friday morning recess and Frenchy St. John threw snowballs at me while the rest of the Indian boys tortured some other *top-yogh-yaught* kid, another weakling. But Frenchy was confident enough to torment me all by himself, and most days I would have let him.
5. But the little warrior in me roared to life that day and knocked Frenchy to the ground, held his head against the snow, and punched him so hard that my knuckles and the snow made symmetrical bruises on his face. He almost looked like he was wearing war paint.
6. But he wasn't the warrior. I was. And I chanted *It's a good day to die, it's a good day to die*, all the way down to the principal's office.

## SECOND GRADE

7. Betty Towle, missionary teacher, redheaded and so ugly that no one ever had a puppy crush on her, made me stay in for recess fourteen days straight.
8. "Tell me you're sorry," she said.
9. "Sorry for what?" I asked.
10. "Everything," she said and made me stand straight for fifteen minutes, eagle-armed with books in each hand. One was a math book; the other was English. But all I learned was that gravity can be painful.

11. For Halloween I drew a picture of her riding a broom with a scrawny cat on the back. She said that her God would never forgive me for that.
12. Once, she gave the class a spelling test but set me aside and gave me a test designed for junior high students. When I spelled all the words right, she crumpled up the paper and made me eat it.
13. "You'll learn respect," she said.
14. She sent a letter home with me that told my parents to either cut my braids or keep me home from class. My parents came in the next day and dragged their braids across Betty Towle's desk.
15. "Indians, indians, indians." She said it without capitalization. She called me "indian, indian, indian."
16. And I said, *Yes, I am. I am Indian. Indian, I am.*

THIRD GRADE

17. My traditional Native American art career began and ended with my very first portrait: Stick Indian Taking a Piss in My Backyard.
18. As I circulated the original print around the classroom, Mrs. Schluter intercepted and confiscated my art.
19. *Censorship*, I might cry now. *Freedom of expression*, I would write in editorials to the tribal newspaper.
20. In third grade, though, I stood alone in the corner, faced the wall, and waited for the punishment to end.
21. I'm still waiting.

FOURTH GRADE

22. "You should be a doctor when you grow up," Mr. Schluter told me, even though his wife, the third grade teacher, thought I was crazy beyond my years. My eyes always looked like I had just hit-and-run someone.
23. "Guilty," she said. "You always look guilty."
24. "Why should I be a doctor?" I asked Mr. Schluter.

25. "So you can come back and help the tribe. So you can heal people."
26. That was the year my father drank a gallon of vodka a day and the same year that my mother started two hundred different quilts but never finished any. They sat in separate, dark places in our HUD house and wept savagely.
27. I ran home after school, heard their Indian tears, and looked in the mirror. *Doctor Victor,* I called myself, invented an education, talked to my reflection. *Doctor Victor to the emergency room.*

FIFTH GRADE

28. I picked up a basketball for the first time and made my first shot. No. I missed my first shot, missed the basket completely, and the ball landed in the dirt and sawdust, sat there just like I had sat there only minutes before.
29. But it felt good, that ball in my hands, all those possibilities and angles. It was mathematics, geometry. It was beautiful.
30. At that same moment, my cousin Steven Ford sniffed rubber cement from a paper bag and leaned back on the merry-go-round. His ears rang, his mouth was dry, and everyone seemed so far away.
31. But it felt good, that buzz in his head, all those colors and noises. It was chemistry, biology. It was beautiful.
32. Oh, do you remember those sweet, almost innocent choices that the Indian boys were forced to make?

SIXTH GRADE

33. Randy, the new Indian kid from the white town of Springdale, got into a fight an hour after he first walked into the reservation school.
34. Stevie Flett called him out, called him a squawman, called him a pussy, and called him a punk.
35. Randy and Stevie, and the rest of the Indian boys, walked out into the playground.

36. “Throw the first punch,” Stevie said as they squared off.
37. “No,” Randy said.
38. “Throw the first punch,” Stevie said again.
39. “No,” Randy said again.
40. “Throw the first punch!” Stevie said for the third time, and Randy reared back and pitched a knuckle fastball that broke Stevie’s nose.
41. We all stood there in silence, in awe.
42. That was Randy, my soon-to-be first and best friend, who taught me the most valuable lesson about living in the white world: *Always throw the first punch.*

SEVENTH GRADE

43. I leaned through the basement window of the HUD house and kissed the white girl who would later be raped by her foster-parent father, who was also white. They both lived on the reservation, though, and when the headlines and stories filled the papers later, not one word was made of their color.
44. *Just Indians being Indians*, someone must have said somewhere and they were wrong.
45. But on the day I leaned through the basement window of the HUD house and kissed the white girl, I felt the goodbyes I was saying to my entire tribe. I held my lips tight against her lips, a dry, clumsy, and ultimately stupid kiss.
46. But I was saying goodbye to my tribe, to all the Indian girls and women I might have loved, to all the Indian men who might have called me cousin, even brother.
47. I kissed that white girl and when I opened my eyes, she was gone from the reservation, and when I opened my eyes, I was gone from the reservation, living in a farm town where a beautiful white girl asked my name.
48. “Junior Polatkin,” I said, and she laughed.
49. After that, no one spoke to me for another five hundred years.

EIGHTH GRADE

50. At the farm town junior high, in the boys' bathroom, I could hear voices from the girls' bathroom, nervous whispers of anorexia and bulimia. I could hear the white girls' forced vomiting, a sound so familiar and natural to me after years of listening to my father's hangovers.
51. "Give me your lunch if you're just going to throw it up," I said to one of those girls once.
52. I sat back and watched them grow skinny from self-pity.
53. Back on the reservation, my mother stood in line to get us commodities. We carried them home, happy to have food, and opened the canned beef that even the dogs wouldn't eat.
54. But we ate it day after day and grew skinny from self-pity.
55. There is more than one way to starve.

NINTH GRADE

56. At the farm town high school dance, after a basketball game in an overheated gym where I had scored twenty-seven points and pulled down thirteen rebounds, I passed out during a slow song.
57. As my white friends revived me and prepared to take me to the emergency room where doctors would later diagnose my diabetes, the Chicano teacher ran up to us.
58. "Hey," he said. "What's that boy been drinking? I know all about these Indian kids. They start drinking real young."
59. Sharing dark skin doesn't necessarily make two men brothers.

TENTH GRADE

60. I passed the written test easily and nearly flunked the driving, but still received my Washington State driver's license on the same day that Wally Jim killed himself by driving his car into a pine tree.
61. No traces of alcohol in his blood, good job, wife and two kids.
62. "Why'd he do it?" asked a white Washington state trooper.

63. All the Indians shrugged their shoulders, looked down at the ground.
64. "Don't know," we all said, but when we look in the mirror, see the history of our tribe in our eyes, taste failure in the tap water, and shake with old tears, we understand completely.
65. Believe me, everything looks like a noose if you stare at it long enough.

ELEVENTH GRADE

66. Last night I missed two free throws which would have won the game against the best team in the state. The farm town high school I play for is nicknamed the "Indians," and I'm probably the only actual Indian ever to play for a team with such a mascot.
67. This morning I pick up the sports page and read the headline: INDIANS LOSE AGAIN.
68. Go ahead and tell me none of this is supposed to hurt me very much.

TWELFTH GRADE

69. I walk down the aisle, valedictorian of this farm town high school, and my cap doesn't fit because I've grown my hair longer than it's ever been. Later, I stand as the school board chairman recites my awards, accomplishments, and scholarships.
70. I try to remain stoic for the photographers as I look toward the future.
71. Back home on the reservation, my former classmates graduate: a few can't read, one or two are just given attendance diplomas, most look forward to the parties. The bright students are shaken, frightened, because they don't know what comes next.
72. They smile for the photographer as they look back toward tradition.
73. The tribal newspaper runs my photograph and the photograph of my former classmates side by side.

### POSTSCRIPT: CLASS REUNION

74. Victor said, "Why should we organize a reservation high school reunion? My graduating class has a reunion every weekend at the Powwow Tavern."

***Sherman Alexie** is a poet, fiction writer, and filmmaker known for witty and frank explorations of the lives of contemporary Native Americans. His stories have been included in several prestigious short story anthologies, including* The Best American Short Stories 2004, *and* Pushcart Prize XXIX. *He is best known for* The Lone Ranger and Tonto Fistfight in Heaven *(1994), a book of short stories, and* Smoke Signals, *a film. Living in Seattle with his wife and children, Alexie occasionally performs as a stand-up comic and holds the record for the most consecutive years as World Heavyweight Poetry Bout Champion.*

# The Torment Haunted Me for Some Time

Roderick Casey II, age 16
Ann Arbor

## FIRST GRADE

I am the youngest of my parents' four children, and the youngest of my father's eight children. Being the youngest kid with four older sisters (I have to live with three of them) is not the best thing for a boy. The amount of bullying and agony weighing on my tiny shoulders was enough to start me on a little journey.

The only place I really felt comfortable was at school. I made a decent amount of friends, but many were the type of friends that had things to say about me behind my back.

One day I got on the bus by myself, since my sisters were sick and at home. I was minding my own business, when some of the older kids began insulting me. Why? I have not the slightest idea.

I did not cry; I did not retaliate with words from my mouth. I kept my lips sealed and waited for my stop. Unfortunately for me, my stop was the last stop.

The torment haunted me for some time.

## FOURTH GRADE

It was after-lunch recess. Usually the fourth graders and third graders would switch off every week, either staying on the little playground or going across the street to the big playground.

This week was the fourth graders' turn to go across the street. A few of them, including me, decided to stay on the little playground while the others went across the street. We stayed on the little playground because it had a basketball court.

The fourth graders started shooting the ball around. We were later joined by a few third-grade boys, and they called a challenge for a basketball game. Of course, back then we used to shoot for team captains, but the third graders already had their minds made up: third graders versus fourth graders. I was not really sure about the whole idea, because every time we separated by grade there was always a conflict minutes later.

About a quarter of an hour into the game, some of the players began to get heated; most of them were fourth graders. Jeremy, one of my teammates, began arguing with the third graders. Two of them argued back. Immediately, I knew they were going to try to fight. The fourth graders held Jeremy back because of three reasons: he was going to fight third graders, we did not want him getting into trouble with the staff, and we would not get the chance to finish our basketball game.

His ignorance began to grow along with his anger. Being the biggest and strongest one, I held Jeremy back. He insisted on trying to swing at one of the little kids. I pulled him away from the court area. His elbow connected to my nose, and blood gushed out. Now I know that it was all an accident.

I grew furious, slamming him against the fence. That is when the proper officials came into play. At that moment, I knew consequences were going to be handed out like candy.

It was a fight that was never even supposed to happen.

TENTH GRADE, SUMMER

Second month of boxing practice.

Nightfall is around the corner. Chilled winds smack against my face. First lap around State Street finished. The second lap begins.

Half an hour later, I enter the gym.

The muggy, moist air hits me.

I hop on the bike for five rounds. Jump rope for five rounds and shadow-box for six rounds. Sparring session is now in play as I take a swig from my water bottle.

Our trainer, Eric, calls me over. He helps me put on my gear.

After putting some Vaseline on my face, I step inside the ring. The bell starts the round as I go after "Bam-Bam," my opponent.

I throw a left-right combination, nothing but a few butterfly love-taps. Bam-Bam throws a left hook.

I catch the hook. He throws a right jab as I knock it away.

He tries for a left jab with a series of combination punches. I slip and get under the punches and retaliate.

A left hook got Bam-Bam stumbling. My back was against the ropes as he fired on me.

I blocked the wild punches while moving away from the ropes and switching up the momentum of the fight. He is now on the ropes.

A left haymaker and a right uppercut knocks his mouth guard out. He stumbles over the middle rope while doubled over.

The round ends.

Confidence is key. I truly float like a butterfly and sting like a bee.

### TENTH GRADE, AUTUMN

It was about a week and a half before Huron High School's homecoming dance. I came back from my boxing class with a surprise for my mother.

Mother was in the kitchen cooking. I walked into the kitchen, stepping foot into the light.

"Hello, Mother," I called to her. My sister Ivana and my father stood beside me, anxious to see Mother's reaction. She turned to me, and her eyes got big.

"Ah!" she shrilled. "My baby!" She finished washing her hands and dried them on a towel. She began examining my black eye. She turned my head from left to right until I jerked back to get out of her grasp. I told her my mistake of bobbing when I should have weaved.

Ice and steak rested on my eye for most of the night.

I woke up the next morning and decided I did not want to go to school. I didn't want to go because I didn't want the students getting the wrong message. To add on to that, I did not feel like explaining myself to a hundred people.

Mother made me go anyway.

I arrived at school, ready to tell my story. Some facial expressions were sorrowful, and some were concerned. Then there were people (the male teachers) that were proud of my black eye—they knew about me taking up boxing.

I probably told the same story twenty or thirty times. I was not embarrassed or shy to speak about my personal experience. I guess that was because I got a black eye doing something productive and not "clowning around" in the streets.

I gained a decent amount of respect (especially from the teachers). The type of response I was getting from the student body and staff was not new to me. The trainers at the boxing gym were also proud of me and my determination.

## ELEVENTH GRADE

My fighting days are practically over. I think I may be getting too old since I dislocated my shoulder twice in two weeks last summer. I have been holding off on the whole boxing situation, but I may go back some time during spring 2010. Lately, I have been doing a different kind of fighting. I am fighting to get my education and to get in the best colleges or universities that I can get into. I was invited to attend a National Youth Leadership Forum in Washington, D.C., where I will be looking into national security and American diplomacy and visiting George Mason University to see what the college is like. Also, I will be given college credit in the subject that I want to major in.

Of course, this is a big opportunity for me; and yes, I am going to attend. The thing is, there are more opportunities for me. I have been invited to attend brunch with the dean at Lawrence Technical University in Southfield, Michigan, and I have received many awards based on my academics. If I continue to play my cards right, fight hard, and maintain my determination to get a great education, there will be more opportunities for me.

This is still fighting, although it is from a different perspective. I'm fighting to become the best that I can be, and hopefully I will be fighting in places such as Washington, D.C.

***Roderick Casey II*** *is the youngest of his mother's four children and his father's eight children. During his senior year, he plans to dual-enroll at Washtenaw Community College. During the mornings, he will be with fourteen other students in Home Building class, where he'll learn how to put up drywall, do electrical work, and install plumbing. For college, Roderick is leaning toward leaving the state. He would like to become a pilot in the Air Force and also study video game design and production. Roderick enjoys singing; playing the drums, bass guitar, and piano; writing; and volunteering for political campaigns. He and his mother have a strong mother-son bond, which is why he is often in such a rush to get home from school.*

# The Contrast

## Maria Roldan, age 17

Ann Arbor

FOURTH GRADE

I was living in Mexico. There was only one week left of school, and our class was having a break. We were eating snacks, and our teacher wanted our attention. She said she was going to announce the students with the best grades in our classroom. We already knew my friend Laura was going to be in first place because she was really smart and had always won first place since the first grade. Just like we thought, Laura was the first name our teacher announced. Then she announced second place: it was my friend Abraham, and there was only one spot left.

"Third place . . . Maria Roldan!" she said. I could not believe it. I was in shock. It was the first time I had won that award, and after that, for the first time, I started to have confidence in myself. I knew if I worked hard I could win more of those awards.

FIFTH GRADE

I had just moved to Michigan from Mexico, and it was my first day of school. Everyone was friendly to me, but I had no clue what they were telling me. I met my teacher and he spoke Spanish well. I felt better that there was at least someone who spoke my own language and someone who really understood me. Mr. Gutierrez was his name. He was really nice and helped me to be more comfortable. It was recess time and I was sitting on the swings, and a girl with curly blond hair smiled at me and approached me.

"Do you want to play with us?" she said. But I didn't answer because I didn't know what she was saying at all. Then she called our teacher over and told him to translate for me. Mr. Gutierrez translated for me what she was saying.

"Her name is Angela. She is asking me if you want to play tag with them?"

"Yes, sure," I said. We started playing tag. After we were done playing, Mr. Gutierrez introduced me to three other boys who were from Mexico, too. I became good friends with them, but I still had trouble understanding. It was hard for me to concentrate because the teacher taught the whole class in English. I didn't pay attention in class at all because I didn't understand.

### SIXTH GRADE

I went to South Arbor Academy for middle school. It was the hardest year yet for me because no one spoke any Spanish at all, not even the teachers or the students. I had to learn everything by myself because they didn't have any ESL classes. I struggled a lot. I was failing all my classes. I was starting to understand more English, but I couldn't speak it at all. I had trouble pronouncing some words, and I would get frustrated not knowing how to say a word correctly so my friends or teachers would understand me.

By December, I understood more of what was happening around me, and I started to communicate more with my classmates. They helped me build my vocabulary by showing me how to pronounce words correctly or by pointing at things and saying their names. Math was easier for me because numbers are like a global language. By the end of the year I was speaking more with my friends, improving my grades, and I had more confidence in myself.

### SEVENTH GRADE

I worked twice as hard, and I tried to improve my grades more. I tried out for the soccer team and made it: I was right forward. We had a great season. We were undefeated throughout the whole season, and then the big final came. We drove all the way to Canton, where our game was going to be. We were so excited; it was our last game of the season.

We started warming up while two other teams played against each other to determine who was going to play against us. Finally the game was over: Canton had beat the other team, and it was our turn to face them.

We started the game just fine, but then Canton scored, and it was 1–0. We were losing, but we kept on fighting. Then they scored again; it was 2–0. We were getting frustrated. Finally, I had the ball. I passed to one of my teammates and she scored! Now the score was 2–1. We were still losing, but we didn't give up. Then my friend Elizabeth took it all the way to the goal and she scored! The score was 2–2, and there were a few minutes left. We were already so tired, but we didn't give up. There were only three minutes left, and we had a corner kick. I was standing close to the goal, so my friend Sarah kicked it and it came toward me. I raised my knee, knocked the ball toward my feet, and kicked it directly toward the goal. We scored! There were a few seconds left, but we were already winning so we started to celebrate. Then they blew the whistle. We started to jump up and down. We were celebrating. Everyone was so happy, and everyone congratulated me for scoring the winning goal. I was so proud of myself and my team.

### TENTH GRADE

Two years after I got my first camera, I started taking pictures with it, mostly when I was with my family or friends. I wasn't that into it, but when I was a freshman I would see pictures that would get my attention: the contrast. What was captured at that moment—I just thought it was awesome.

I'm a quiet person, and shy at times. I don't like to talk in front of people, but I think drawing and taking pictures is a good way to express myself. I like to observe things that represent something. I get attracted by things that have contrast.

I started researching how photographers make their pictures look so good. I downloaded different types of photo software. Some of them were hard to use, but I started to play around with them and I got better at it. I started to take pictures and edit them by adding contrast, words, and different colors. I started to get into the photography world more and more, and I decided to take photo classes at my school. I learned so much in my photography class, like how to make a camera out of cardboard that could take actual black-and-white pictures. I also got to work in a darkroom where photographers develop their pictures by using an enlarger and chemicals to develop film. I decided to take Photography II in my first semester of eleventh grade.

I enjoy taking pictures and editing them. I can find myself doing this for hours and never get tired or bored. I've decided to learn more about it and hopefully get a photography job in the future because it's something I really enjoy doing.

***Maria Roldan*** *was born in Mexico and came to America when she was nine years old. She has a younger sister attending primary school. In her free time she likes to listen to music, draw, paint, play soccer, and take pictures and edit them. She is graduating this year and is really excited. She plans to take photo classes in college, get a good education, and be successful in life.*

# Public Schools in San Francisco

Jessica Barrog, age 17
San Francisco

### NEVER TRUST A TALKING GIRAFFE

I remember erasing all the R's that I spent an entire *Rugrats* episode carefully crafting. I wrote them all backward. Thanks a lot, Toys 'Я' Us. Never trust a talking giraffe. I stuck my lips through the holes where the paper had thinned and blew raspberries at Derek, the cootie-infested boy sitting across from me. He stuck his pencil in my mouth the third—and last—time I did it.

### BELLY BUTTON BLUFF

I wore a red-checkerboard bathing suit top and water shoes to class, explaining it was because I had won free tickets to go to Raging Waters after school. Raging Waters isn't open in December, and I was terrified of water slides. The truth was I had already worn all my shirts that week and the rest were at my dad's house. I didn't want my friends to know my parents were divorced. They found out later, when my toothbrush fell out of my backpack and I was out of lies.

### DON'T FROST YOUR CAKE WITH LOTION

My teacher kept a big tub of hand lotion next to the chalkboard. I was dared to eat it. I scooped up the lotion like Betty Crocker frosting and plunged my fingers into my mouth. Drool surged from the sides of my tongue to wash down the bitter cream. I spit it out in huge wads, but the lotion stuck like napalm. I wondered if I was going to throw up. I wondered if my tongue would dissolve and my face would collapse into my throat and I'd turn into a dust bunny. But instead, I had to sit in time-out for "wasting resources," and gagged all the way to recess.

### STEP ASIDE, LISA FRANK

Sydney, Stephanie, and Meghan all had psychedelic Lisa Frank folders with rainbow cowgirls and ballerina bunnies. My folder was navy blue and said "Bank of America" in taunting gold letters. I ripped my folder up and brought it home to my mother. After I told her it got run over by three buses and a green motorcycle, she duct-taped it back together, telling me that I'd have to do better than that. I stopped using folders, so my teacher gave me one of hers. The whole third grade thought it was the coolest folder because Ms. Green got it for me from SCRAP, her favorite store. I didn't know what SCRAP was, but it was the most exquisite black folder I'd ever owned.

### A TALENTED WHITE WATERMELON

The last year I had to learn Chinese. Every Tuesday, for thirty minutes, we would do Chinese brush painting on expensive rice paper. My appointed Chinese name, if pronounced incorrectly, was White Watermelon (Bat Soy Gua instead of Bak Sai Ga). The boys in Room 212 never found an end to the hilarious abyss of jokes they would spit at me for this name. Revenge came when Ms. Chang made fun of their watery, bloated bamboo sticks after praising my painting; her "Ay yah!" electrocuted their slouched spines into perfect posture.

### TRAINING FOR SOMETHING BIGGER

I was already wearing a training bra. It was blue with white stripes and a cartoon monkey in the middle—voted by my friends as the cutest training bra in existence. Comparing mine to their black-and-white hand-me-down training bras, I had to agree. We had sex ed at the end of the year. All the boys sat on one side while the girls sat on the other. I'd say it was like a school dance, but I didn't know what those were yet. When Mr. Sheen talked about periods, he smiled at me. After that, everyone thought I had gotten my period—which I hadn't—and I was careful not to go to the bathroom during class for the next couple of weeks. Having your period at that age was like telling people you watched porn—with your grandmother.

### MS. POPULAR

I carried around a backpack so enormous and tightly stuffed that the big zipper busted open while I walked home from school. I scrambled to pick up loose papers but lost my Wednesday envelope. My homeroom teacher gave me a grade of U (unsatisfactory) for the semester. Her room number was 324. The square root of 324 is 18. And 18 = 6+6+6, and her last name was Helliskov. Was it a coincidence? I never thought so, but I had too much free time. That same year, I reached level 24 in Tetris and started a collection of my chewed gum. I wasn't lonely. Lots of people were my friends. They just didn't know it yet.

### WHAT A CUBE HEAD

My math teacher gave us an unsolved Rubik's Cube as an assignment. We had a week, but by the fifth day my cube was in worse shape than when I started. I gave this quiet Chinese boy named Marcus five packs of Gushers to fix it for me. He fixed it in two minutes and sixteen seconds. I was one of the four in the class that had finished the task successfully, including Marcus. When the teacher asked me how I fixed it, I laughed nervously and replied, "You know, how does anyone fix these things? I just did it." He shook his head and gave me a medium-hard Sudoku sheet and told me that it was for me to do, not Marcus.

### LOCK UP THE SHARPIES

Anastasia thought it would be funny to write in black Sharpie all over my arm. I wasn't paying attention to what she was doing; I was reading *I Know Why the Caged Bird Sings* like a normal student. Anastasia wasn't a normal student. She liked to throw erasers at my forehead because she "felt like it" and flirt with our forty-year-old teacher. When Mr. Gregwith saw my arm, he made me scrub it until my skin was as red as Anastasia's bloodshot eyes. She brought chocolate-chip cookies to school that day; inside them were "nuggets of herbal goodness," according to the skateboarders. Everyone took a bite except me.

### FRESHMAN FRIDAY, GALILEO HIGH SCHOOL, 2007

Time of day: 0800 hours. All was quiet on the first floor. Three troop-members were wounded in the main office. The enemy had strategically placed garbage cans in the middle of the hallway on the second and third floors. During break, sophomores and juniors banged on these cans, the racket shivering from one small body to the next. I banged on these cans too and walked like a hungry mountain lion. I thought I was slick, but I was wearing the bright purple and orange wristband they gave to all ninth graders. It read "Galileo Class of 2011." I stripped it off my wrist so fast it left a ring of raw skin. I pulled my sleeve over my hand before I could be discovered. They're in cahoots with the faculty, I thought. I tried to burn it but it wouldn't catch fire. It was like Gollum's ring. I left the battlefield three weeks later, for the peaceful land of School of the Arts. I bet that wristband is still in my old locker.

### THE KNOCKOFF VERSION OF BEN AND JERRY'S

In chemistry we had to make our own ice cream. I'm lactose-intolerant, so my group kindly decided to use rice milk. Don't try this at home. After forty-five minutes of shaking a slippery bag of ice, we excitedly revealed our ice cream to the class. I swallowed a huge spoonful, expecting Ben and Jerry's. Somehow the ice cream turned out to be salty, half-frozen, and chunky. The memory of hand lotion triggered my gag reflexes. The other groups were successful and gloated about their decadent chocolate swirl or their volcanic vanilla bean. We gave the rest of our ice cream to our teacher, a teacher that made Marcie cry last year. We left before we could see her purple and twisted scowl, or in case she decided to throw the jar at us.

HEATHER WOODWARD: TEACHER, MOTHER, HERO

My teacher fell off the stage at our performance. She suffered a concussion, but managed to wake up in character and finish the show. Her husband carted her away to the hospital afterward. I've never seen a more convincing rendition of a homeless man on a bus in my life. She even had fake tattoo sleeves on her arms. When she came backstage to say good-bye, sweat dripped from her forehead like the tears she wouldn't cry in front of us. I watched the beads slowly outline her face, and decided that she was the best teacher I would ever have.

***Jessica Barrog** is a high school senior in the creative writing department at the San Francisco School of the Arts High School. Her work has been published in* Sliver of Stone Magazine; *in* Spirit Magazine; *in the school's literary journal,* Umlaut; *and on protestpoems.org. She aspires to make people laugh because humor is often forgotten in difficult times such as these.*

# School Is for Learning

## Nola McCue, age 17
San Francisco

### FIRST GRADE: LEARNING THAT ADULTS CAN BE STUPID, TOO

"Nola is a bright and engaging child," Maria stated. "However, one thing about her is causing me concern." Maria was my first-grade teacher. She was strict, abrasive, and uncompromising.

"What's wrong?" my father asked.

"She reads all the time."

"And that's a problem?" my mother interjected. "She likes to read."

Now they were embroiled in this discussion. Mother and Maria were both opinionated and stubborn. This would not end until one grown-up's argument was left bleeding on the classroom floor.

"She doesn't do much else during free time."

"It is called free time, Maria. The whole premise is that she should be allowed to do what she chooses. So what if she'd rather read than play with plastic dinosaurs?"

"We'd like her to vary the activities she takes part in, Mrs. McCue. She shows a lack of interest in other pursuits."

"Maybe she doesn't find them interesting."

"We'd like Nola to receive a more well-rounded education."

"Then maybe you should become a more well-rounded educator."

"Thank you, Maria," my father butted in, hoping to end this conflict before it evolved into all-out war. He stood up, shook Maria's hand, and ushered my mother out of the room. Mama was fuming. I've heard you could practically see hot, gray steam rising from each of her pores after that meeting.

Mama didn't tell me about this conversation until I was old enough to recognize its value, the ironic injustice of it. When she did, I was immediately frustrated by its stupidity. The irritation collected in a pinpoint, causing a sort of hot, itchy feeling of my soul, concentrated between my collarbones. Why would that woman think that my childhood love of literature was a stumbling block in my development? Almost as fast as the annoyance absorbed me, it subsided. I let all the hatred of my first-grade nemesis trickle down into my stomach, where it was overtaken by the acid.

### SECOND GRADE: LEARNING THAT THE WORLD'S NOT ALWAYS NICE

"You fat cow," a now faceless, nameless fourth grader sneered at me. "When's the baby due?"

I bit back tears with the back of my throat, my soft palate tightening and my teeth clenched hard. In elementary school being pretty doesn't make you special, but if you aren't, you face merciless ridicule for your imperfections.

I didn't understand back then why it was not okay to look the way I did, but I did know that it was a very, very bad thing. I longed to be like everyone else. At that time I believed in God and I prayed to him to make me pretty. I became hyper-attentive when ads for diet pills came on TV. At seven years old, I was already a promising future basket case.

"You didn't answer me. When's that baby coming?"

I clenched my teeth harder. I imagined solid concrete dams in each of my eyes, holding back the torrent of waterworks that threatened to expose me to further ridicule. It was just one incident in a string of incidents that helped me become what I would be for a long time. But how could my tormentor or I know that the teasing and insecurity would morph over the next few years into months of watery eyes and stomach acid in my throat? And all for the chance to be like everyone else.

If he had known he had the power to do that to me, it wouldn't have mattered. The ridicule was my real grade-school education. By the time I reached middle school, hating my flaws was a part of me, much more ingrained in me than addition, subtraction, or multiplication would ever be. Academics were not a facet of my personality, but feeling terrible about myself was. In time I would learn to love myself, however, just as I had been taught self-hatred.

## FOURTH GRADE: LEARNING TO HANDLE DISAPPOINTMENT

Noreen Tierney really loved us, and we loved her right back. She was the first really engaging teacher any of us had ever had. Because of her work, we were sent on scores of field trips. She did all she had to, working for grants so we could participate in the Marin Headlands overnight field trips and taking us on trips to the Dolphin Club, where her husband would take two children at a time out on the bay in their tiny rowboat. They loved boats and the bay so much that they lived on a little houseboat named Anabel.

On this particular occasion, we were supposed to camp out in a lighthouse in Marin whose name I can no longer recall. We had gotten permission slips signed, bought new sleeping bags, and prepared our meal for the next night (there would be no way to get food once we were there). The morning we were to leave, every one of us showed up bright-eyed and excited. That was when our student teacher showed up in the yard to lead us into the room with a look on her face like something had gone wrong.

Up in our classroom we were told that the field trip we had looked forward to would not happen. Our beloved teacher could not make it that day.

"Ms. Tierney is too sick to come today," the student teacher said, trying her best to look concerned. Her eyes told us she didn't much care. "She has very bad food poisoning."

"What made her sick?" a student asked solemnly, mourning his field trip.

"She ate some bad meat."

I was a vegetarian for four years after that.

### SIXTH GRADE: LEARNING TO STAND OUT

Mr. Johnson was a very sarcastic man. He infused his dry wit with a self- (and everybody-else-) deprecating nasal tone. I entered his orchestra class four days late, having been erroneously placed in the general arts classes. Everybody gave me strange, hostile looks. Nobody knew me, and, as I was about to discover, I was sitting in somebody else's seat. I had chosen to sit in the back, hoping to avoid being singled out for any reason on my first day of orchestra class. Inevitably, I was singled out as the only person there for the first time on the fourth day of school.

"Your name, please?" he asked in a voice reminiscent of Squidward, a character on a then wildly popular cartoon show.

"Nola McCue?" I said, not really asking a question but so nervous that my every word seemed like one.

"What do you play?"

"Violin?"

"How long have you been playing?"

"Since I was five?"

The class murmured. They had all started at eight because that was when elementary school music programs started.

"Come to the front of the class, Ms. McCue."

No. No. No! My palms grew sticky with sweat and crumpled under the strength of my forming fists. I was hoping to avoid this. I didn't want to sit anywhere near the front of the orchestra. I wanted to sit in the back and play my violin and not be noticed. My middle school was full of people who had gone to elementary school together in the Richmond, and I had gone to school in the Mission, leaving me out of everyone's groups again. Standing out was not a good thing to add to my situation.

Instead of objecting, I stood up, picked up my stuff, and moved to the seat in the front. Mr. Johnson gave me an encouraging nod. Later, I realized that nod was the closest thing to a compliment he would ever give me, and at that point he hadn't even heard me play. The more I thought about this new situation, the less I feared sitting up front. Maybe it was about time all my practicing got me recognition.

### NINTH GRADE: LEARNING TO REALLY LOVE YOUR FRIENDS

We spent eleven hours on the bus. That's two hours longer than it ever took to go the same distance in my friend's tiny car, but I suppose that three buses full of teenagers have to make pit stops more often. We were L.A.-bound, emerging triumphant from the San Francisco fog to conquer other high school music programs.

The problem with conquering other music programs is that sometimes they conquer us back, and the problem with putting a bunch of teenagers together on a bus for eleven hours is just obvious. There was the usual stupid high school drama, as well as a student running through and shattering the glass doors of the hotel the night after we arrived. It was one of the more uneventful overnight trips.

The tour taught me to really love the people I experienced it with. I literally spent one night laughing and the next night sobbing with the girls in my hotel room. We learned way more than we needed to know about each other over the course of four days, becoming closer friends than we thought we would be after four years together.

***Nola McCue** lives with her parents, two cats, and a geriatric dog. When she isn't writing stories about her childhood, you can probably find her dancing or playing her guitar on the street for tips. She has always wanted to be a doctor but can't because she's so puke-phobic.*

# A New Beginning

Janice Campbell, age 16
Boston

FIFTH GRADE: ABANDON

I don't remember this teacher's name. I only know that he was male. He was only there for the first two months of school and then he disappeared. There were rumors that he took a couple of days off and went out of town. Others said he got fired, and the boys in class said he ran away because he was wanted by the police. I don't know what his reason was and I don't care. He should have at least told us he was leaving.

But that year was mad fun. No teacher—only substitutes. We barely did any work; we did what we wanted to do, no questions asked. No rules, no nothing. We were living it up, but when the time came to take the MCAS, we all suffered for his mistake. Aren't teachers always supposed to be there for their students?

EIGHTH GRADE: I'M A PARADOX

I was a bully. I was scared of nothing and no one. The only time anyone saw me smile was when I was with my twin and Toni and the boys; that was it. Besides that, I was always mugging someone. People who didn't know me would automatically assume I was mean because of "that face," and some said that when I smiled, I looked evil. That face was just a front to scare people off, to let them know that I wasn't to be messed with. I got into a lot of fights that year—

seven, to be exact. There were only three that the principal knew about, and I was only suspended for two of those fights.

I had four fights on the school bus, one in the music room, one in the locker room, and one in the bathroom. The other girls in my class and I were bored, so we decided to have a fight in the bathroom. During lunch, each girl had to pair up with another and fight, and whoever won had to pair up with another girl who had won another fight, and so on. The fight in the music room was basically a rematch of one of the fights that had happened on the school bus, with a girl named Shonnysha.

The boys thought we should have a rematch because they didn't know who was telling the truth about winning. I told them no, because I wasn't trying to get suspended again. But they didn't care: they had a little plan of their own. When we were in music class they started pushing Shonnysha and me into each other. When I turned around to tell one of the boys to stop, I felt Shonnysha push me. So I turned around and pushed her back, and then she slapped me. When she slapped me, my glasses flew off my face. I looked at her, and then at my glasses, and I grabbed her by her hair. After that I just blacked out.

I came back to reality when the school police officer grabbed me and pulled me off her. I didn't even remember what happened; the boys told me that I had won. When I looked around, I saw Shonnysha standing by the door holding her nose. Then she looked up at me. She had a bloodshot eye, and her nose was bleeding. All I know about the fight is what I was told. The rest is just a mystery. Why is it that people always try and test your patience, even if they already know not to mess with you?

### NINTH GRADE: A NEW BEGINNING

Another new school. I couldn't stay at the old one; they were trying to hold me back a grade. I had never been held back before, so I told my mom I wanted to go to a regular public school—charter schools weren't working out for me.

The first day, I made friends—all boys, of course. They showed me to my classes, and they were the people I hung out with for the next couple of days, but they were freshmen, so I had to get to know the upperclassmen. That all happened in two days, so I had my new group of friends and everything was going fine—until I was in math class and the teacher was teaching something I'd never seen before but should've known. I was sitting there feeling dumb because I had no clue what he was talking about and I had no clue how to do the work. I thought: *This is all my mom's fault. If she'd put me in a regular school I would know what the teacher was talking about. But no, she wanted me to go to a charter school where they forgot to teach some important stuff, and now I'm sitting here looking dumb.*

This happened in a lot of my other classes, too, and I started to fall behind in basically every subject except English. I wasn't used to how the teachers taught, and half of the stuff they talked about I didn't know or even understand. I didn't want to ask for help because I didn't want to single myself out, and also because I didn't want them to think that I needed to go back to the ninth grade. If that happened, I would truly have a heart attack and die.

Why don't parents ever listen to their children? Why do they feel like they always need to be right about everything?

***Janice Campbell** is a student at the English High School in Boston, where she was born and raised. She hopes to become more independent—and, eventually, a nurse—and is excited to finish high school within a year.*

# Social Birthplace

Daryn Gethers, age 18
Boston

FIRST GRADE: THE BRIGHTEST

Orangeburg, South Carolina

Starting first grade was something I looked forward to. I was a bright young male with the passion to learn but a tendency to play around. I was the smartest person in all my classes, but I failed the majority of my tests—in everything but math. I would know every answer but wouldn't speak up out of fear of being wrong—or being right. I didn't want to be wrong because that's just how I was. I didn't want to be right because then I would be classified as a nerd. The teachers started to take note of my keen sense with math—and my lack of courage to share what I knew when they saw that I did no classwork but made 90s on the tests.

EIGHTH GRADE: STAYING OUT OF TROUBLE

Orangeburg, South Carolina

It's Friday. I've almost completed the first week of eighth grade. School gets out at 3:30, and, at 3:23, I get into a fight.

Everybody is in science class throwing spitballs. Even though they're spitting paper at each other, none of the students gets mad. There are spitballs on my desk and on the floor around me. The teacher tells me to pick up the spitballs off the floor. I tell her, "No!"

She gets loud and threatens to write me up. I tell her I wasn't throwing spitballs at myself, so I'm not picking them up.

This fat kid, who was throwing spitballs along with everyone else, busts out, "All I know is, you better not say it was me!"

I look at him and tell him, "I didn't say anyone did it." He repeats it and my anger flares. I ball up a sheet of paper as I walk toward him.

"I didn't say you did it!" I'm yelling now as I throw the paper in his face. He pushes me while he is still sitting. I punch him. His head slams into the wall, and I take a step back. He swings with power, but way too slowly. I easily block his fist and wrap my left hand around his neck, beating his face with my right hand.

That was a great year.

### NINTH GRADE: CORRUPTION

Orangeburg, South Carolina

Orangeburg Wilkerson High School: I was a freshman, class of 2010, wandering the halls in search of friends and my new classes. I went to class every day. One day I was late to class and I wasn't allowed in. I had to skip, and I was nervous. My friends who skipped told me to take it easy, but I got caught later that day. Even though I got caught, I liked the thrill and I did it again. I spent at least half the year skipping school. When I got bored, I skipped. It was something to do. I soon got bored of that and wanted to let the administrators know I was skipping. I liked to run from them, knowing they would never catch me.

### NINTH GRADE (AGAIN): CORRUPTION, PART 2

Orangeburg, South Carolina

Orangeburg Wilkerson High School: I was a freshman again, class of 2011. At first I was on the right path, actually going to school and doing work, but that got boring, so I started skipping again. One day, while I was skipping school, I broke into what I thought was an abandoned house with my best friend since eighth grade, Nick. We entered the house—but then saw a bed and TV, so we got out quickly. When we were behind the house, the cops spotted us. We ran behind houses, eluding trees, stumps, and gates. We were getting cornered. I told Nick to jump the barbed-wire fence. Nick was halfway over and asked, "Where are they?" I looked back and they were coming, full speed. I ran back and pushed him over the gate and told him to run. He hesitated at first but saw the uniforms and knew I wouldn't want him to get caught just because I did. He ran and escaped.

Two policemen came around the house from opposite sides and yelled, "Freeze!" I looked both ways as they lunged for me. I turned my back to the gate and did a half run, half crawl under the house to the other side. I was too fast; soon, they were out of the picture. Three more policemen were chasing me. I cut right, and an officer lost his footing. I jumped fence after fence, not looking back, the sound of branches breaking behind me. I was too tired to last much longer when I saw one more gate—so close to freedom. Then four cop cars and two trucks sped in and blocked my way. I was too tired to give the cars the proper chase they deserved. I gave up and got locked up.

After I got out, I was forced to move to Boston with my dad. That was mid-April in 2008, during my second freshman year. I was mad because I had to go to school for an extra month. I knew only two people when I came to English High, Rashad and Kenny, but I made friends pretty quickly after people saw me play basketball and realized how fast I was.

***Daryn Gethers*** *is a high school senior in Boston who is originally from Orangeburg, South Carolina. He's a passionate basketball player and cook who values his family and community. Daryn became a proud published author in 2010, with the release of* Small Things Can Grow Tall, *a book by his high school class that was published by 826 Boston.*

# Transition

## Marco Madera, age 17

Boston

FIRST GRADE: I'M A BIG KID NOW

Lincoln, Massachusetts

I felt like a big kid, kind of. One day at lunch, Jimmy threw a piece of sandwich at me because I was sitting at the girls' table, being cool as usual. I got up and pushed him off his seat and smacked him in the face. He cried.

That was the first time a teacher said, "Oh, Marco," but it was not the last.

THIRD GRADE: DANCIN' FOOL

Lincoln, Massachusetts

I remember third grade like it was yesterday. That was the year I went to the sock hop with little Suzy May. That was the year that teachers collected homework regularly, and if I forgot to do it I used the ever-popular "My dog ate it" or "I lost it on the bus" excuse. Yep, sometimes the teacher would get so mad that her face would turn Mercury-red and her eyes would look like golf balls of fury. The consequences were simple, though: a call home or no recess. I didn't mind because life was sweet.

FIFTH GRADE: RELATIONS

Lincoln, Massachusetts

"Cool," I said after asking a girl out for the first time. She'd actually said yes. I was happy. This year I felt like the big man in the schoolyard because I had a girlfriend. We ate lunch, sat on the bench during recess, and held hands in line while leaving school to get on the bus—until I ate her Oreos. She dumped me. She said, "Oh Marco . . ." and I went home. It was a good two days, anyway.

### NINTH GRADE: FRESH MEAT

Boston, Massachusetts

Freshman year: oh, great—I don't like remembering this year. This year was about popularity and style. I kind of kept my geeky ways and chilled with the weird people, better known as my friends. Ty, Max, and I played guitar every spare moment we had, sang at lunch, and tried to play off the loser shake we all had among us.

I'm going to be straight about this year: my "Oh, Marco" moment was when I skipped a scheduled class every day. I only skipped it because it wasn't a class; it was like a homework help session. It was stupid, I felt sad going to it, and I didn't need it. So I skipped and had detention every other day. Instead, I went into the band room, grabbed a guitar, and played with my friends.

"Oh, me."

### TENTH GRADE: TRANSITION

Boston, Massachusetts

This year I brought my grades up a bit. I had a good three semesters overall, until I transferred schools during the last semester. It was all right with me, because things seemed fine. That is, until I had my first substitute. He seemed like a normal, laid-back guy, and the kids seemed to have some respect for him. But once that door closed and class started, all hell broke loose—kids asking the teacher, "Hey, did you vote for Hitler?" and "Sir, are you still single?"

The students played card games, and the substitute had a long *Why on earth am I here?* look on his face as he sat at the desk. I wondered if it was normal to treat a substitute this way at this school, and I was informed that it surely was.

I could tell that the next couple of years were going to be interesting.

***Marco Madera** still misses the go-kart he had as a child. He is now a high school senior in Boston and cannot wait to attend college and see new places. He says, "I don't have any wishes or hopes, just goals," a testament to his self-assuredness and determination. He would like to thank his mother for everything.*

# Back to Basics

## Elizabeth (Ellie) Nguyen, age 16

Boston

FIRST GRADE: EVERYTHING IS GOOD BY THE BAE
Boston, Massachusetts

Today was the first day of the first grade: the first day to set a foundation for the rest of my life. I merrily skipped through the little classroom door that read, "Welcome to the Paul A. Dever Elementary School! Mrs. Bae, Grade 1," which, at the time, I thought just said, "Enter."

I was like the sun and had a gravitational pull on people, like planets. I ran my mouth as if I had shoes for teeth. People always seemed to be interested in what I had to say. But when the teacher told me to stand in front and introduce myself, I froze. The pomegranate I had for breakfast must've seeped through my gums because they now stained my chubby cheeks. I couldn't even remember the name that was bestowed upon me when I took my first breath. Was I afraid to show them who I was? Did I look stupid just standing there?

"Elizabeth," I finally said. "I was named after the queen!"

Mrs. Bae chuckled a bit and bowed. "Well, it's an honor to meet you, Your Highness." I knew I was going to like her.

I was then introduced to twenty-six little possibilities that would stick with me forever. There were endless things you could do with A–Z, and infinite new memories to make with my new best friend, Nhien Dao. We were like little old ladies; we gossiped about previous years we could barely remember. To many people we were Siamese twins. Going down the slides, lying on the rug, eating the inedible—we were inseparable.

SEVENTH GRADE: OREO EPIPHANY
Boston, Massachusetts

Lunch was just beginning, and it was another typical day at Boston Latin Academy. I sat down and said "hi" as conversations started to drift on their own. I held an Oreo between my fingers and scanned the people at my table: Linh, Jenny, Mina, Matt, Jimmy, and Trang. What else did I really know about these people? I looked through the whole cafeteria and saw how divided we all were. "Why am I sitting here?" I thought. "I really don't even like these people." I looked up at the room again and realized we all shared nothing with the people at our tables besides a place of origin. I stared at the Oreo again. If black and white could come together here and be something so wonderful, it was time for me to become my own Oreo. I sat down with another girl and complimented her on how well her outfit matched her icy blue eyes. Madeline and I have been best friends ever since.

NINTH GRADE: A TASTE OF SOVEREIGNTY
Medford, Massachusetts

My pupils dilated as the spotlight hit me, and all I could hear was my heartbeat after the music had stopped. "And now presenting the first freshman in Medford High history to become Homecoming Queen: Ellie Nguyen!" The smile I wore was a true result of manifest destiny: it had the divine right to spread from one side of my face to the other. I officially had it all. I was the president of the 2011 class, co-captain of the volleyball team, and coordinator of the Key Club. I also had the perfect boyfriend, the Homecoming King. He was captain of the football team, and everyone gave me what I wanted because they were afraid of him. He was a tower, and the team was a city. Nothing could ruin this night. I was surrounded by all the people I loved, letting my worries fade with every step I took. That night set a precedent for the rest of the year. It was the best year of my life.

ELEVENTH GRADE: LEARNING BASIC ENGLISH

Boston, Massachusetts

"Welcome to English High!" I heard for the millionth time that day. I'd moved back to Boston, back to basics. I'd heard so many things about this school; I've never been quick to judge, but the metal detectors weren't doing so much for the school's image in my mind. I was an outcast here. Everybody had his or her fresh-fitteds and dope kicks, things I had given up on a long time ago. They were the kind of people you see in the media, the kind of people you hear on the radio. They cared too much about fitting in and following the latest trends. I wasn't going to change myself to be liked though. I was going to do all I could and make the best with the cards I'd been dealt. *Maybe I'll like this school*, I thought. I took a deep breath and read the sign on the big blue double doors: "Welcome to English High! Home of the blue and blue."

***Elizabeth (Ellie) Nguyen** is a high school senior in Boston. She is a born mentor and an excellent student who wants to study urban planning and international affairs. During the 2009–10 school year, Ellie worked as a teen tutor at 826 Boston, where she assisted younger students with their writing and co-led the editorial board in a publishing project at her own school titled* Small Things Can Grow Tall. *She has seven older siblings.*

# Empty

## Kylie Perry, age 18

Boston

### FIRST GRADE: WHO TO BLAME

Billerica, Massachusetts

Streams ran down my innocent face. "Was this my fault?" I found myself asking repeatedly. It must have been.

"Your mother and I are getting a divorce, kids." He carelessly threw the words at us.

I remember my brother collapsing to the floor and beginning to cry. Nobody told us that it wasn't our fault.

My mother won custody. Although things did not get better overnight, I kept hoping they would. My teacher kept a smile on her face and always had sympathy for me. I would stay after school on some days and talk to her about my family issues, and she always made me feel better. She wasn't only nice to me; she was a nice person overall. I passed with an easy A.

### SECOND GRADE: SNAKE FAIRY

Billerica, Massachusetts

One day after school, I got a pet snake. A couple of months later it died, and for some strange reason I wore it around my neck for weeks. It was fine jewelry. I wore it to grocery stores, restaurants, and more. The smell was unbearable.

"Get that damn snake off your neck!" my mom would shriek.

When my mother could no longer stand the smell, she told me the snake fairy took it away. I didn't cry that time.

ELEVENTH GRADE: EMPTY
Boston, Massachusetts

I skipped school more than I attended. I stayed back in eleventh grade. My family didn't care because my two older brothers had dropped out. I went back anyway. It was easy in a way, because I wanted it for myself. It was also hard because I didn't have to. Does that make sense? Nobody was there when I came home to tell me I was doing the right thing, so why did I keep going to school? These days, when I arrive at my house, it looks empty. Nobody is there. Nothing hangs on the walls. No family pictures. Even the fridge is empty. At least the classroom is full.

***Kylie Perry*** *is a high school senior of Irish and Albanian descent. She plays many sports, including soccer and softball, and is an avid animal lover. Her first snake-owning experience is recounted in the 826 Boston collection* Small Things Can Grow Tall.

# My First Teacher Crush

Alexis Polanco, age 18
Boston

FIRST GRADE: THE BEGINNING OF MY EDUCATION
Mattapan, Massachusetts

I woke up, took a shower, and put on my laid-out clothes.

"Are you ready?" my mother asked my older brother and me.

We responded, "Yeah!" before putting on our backpacks.

The school-arrival jitters tormented me as I refused my breakfast sandwich. On the bus ride, I sat quietly. We approached the school, and I felt like the butterflies in my stomach wanted to burst out, but I tamed them. As I walked up to the school, I could only hear my thoughts and the voice of my brother as he tried to comfort me. My brother helped me to my class, and I wondered what my teacher would be like. Well, there she was, a tall, young, pale-skinned woman with short black hair. "Hey, she doesn't look that bad," I thought—but I was wrong!

The next day came quickly; steps away from the Mattahunt Elementary School, I thought, *Damn! I forgot to do my homework!* As I walked toward my classroom, I couldn't stop shaking from nervousness. I didn't know if that was a real word, but that's what I called it: uncontrollable nervousness. As the day continued I hoped that she'd forget or that the day would be over, but before I knew it, she was asking me for my homework.

"Uhhhhhhh. . . ." I hesitated, but I couldn't come up with an excuse. Finally I answered, "I don't have it."

"What?" she asked.

"I don't have it," I repeated.

"This is unacceptable," she said as she towered over me, rage blazing in her eyes.

### SECOND GRADE: MY FIRST TEACHER CRUSH

Mattapan, Massachusetts

Second grade was nothing like the first. As I stepped into class, I couldn't help but smile. In seven years of life, I had never seen a person light up a room the way she did. Every time I talked to her, I couldn't help but wear a smile from ear to ear. *This is going to be a good year for me*, I told myself every day. She was my reason to get up in the morning that year.

### THIRD GRADE: LIGHTNING MATH

Mattapan, Massachusetts

*I'm an expert at going to school*, I thought as I walked to school. I was used to the environment. I took one look at my teacher and thought it would be first grade all over again—but I learned that appearances can be deceiving.

I remember I enjoyed third grade a lot. My teacher was a lot like Izma from the movie *The Emperor's New Groove*, but her name was Mrs. Duran. The character Izma is very skinny and kind of hunchbacked, with skin sliding off her bones. She was wrinkly and could have easily been 150 years old. Mrs. Duran was Izma, but she was also the teacher who put my mathematical skills to the test, and I always prevailed.

Mrs. Duran would always give my class a quiz of one hundred multiplication questions. "You have five minutes to complete this quiz."

I'd prepare myself.

"Ready . . . and . . . go!"

I'd zoom through those questions like a police car trying to catch a runaway criminal! When I finished, I would slam my pencil down to show I had finished. "Done!" I'd scream out loud, with time to spare.

"One hundred! Great work, Alexis!"

I smiled and thought, *I live for this.*

## FOURTH GRADE: I THINK YOU NEED GLASSES

Mattapan, Massachusetts

This year started the same as all the others. The night before, I stayed up almost all night. That morning, I got up and got ready. By now, the only words out of my mother's mouth were "Hurry up before you miss the bus!"

As I walked to the bus stop, I thought what I always did: *I wonder who my teacher is and who's going to be in my class; hopefully, there will be some of the same students as last year.* My brother and I got on the bus and soon arrived at school.

"See you later," I said to my brother.

As I turned to him, he looked at me and replied with a simple "All right," and we went on with the day.

I walked into class and thought to myself, *Where's the teacher?* As I waited, I walked and looked around the classroom. I stumbled upon a comic strip taped to the wall and laughed at its humor.

A hand landed on my shoulder. "I drew that—and, by the way, I'm Mr. Collins."

"I'm Alexis Polanco," I replied.

As the year continued, I noticed I was struggling. I couldn't see what my teacher was writing on the board, and as the days went by it wasn't getting any better. One day, Mr. Collins walked up to me after class and said, "Alexis, I think you might need to get some glasses." I just remember looking at him and thinking, *This guy is crazy if he thinks I'm going to wear glasses.*

## FIFTH GRADE: MATURITY

Mattapan, Massachusetts

Here we are, in fifth grade, the big-kid role models. We had way more responsibility than everyone else in the school—the leaders, almost in middle school. I was not fazed by the thought. I reacquainted myself with my friends and even made some new ones, but the biggest change in fifth grade was my teacher.

She looked like she was related to the leprechauns. She made sure everything in our agenda books was up to date, all assignments were done, and everyone was on task. If not, there were always repercussions. Other teachers would go get their students from lunch and bring them to class, but she trusted us enough to let us come to class on our own.

One day, she was giving her lesson, and we watched as she struggled to reach for the middle of the board. As she wrote, we heard a sound. We all knew what it was. As everyone laughed, I heard someone say, "Excuse me," in a monotone voice. All I could think was, *Classic!*

NINTH GRADE: FRESHMAN BEAT DOWN
Jamaica Plain, Massachusetts

It's Day One. The doors creak open. It's like a Western. I look from left to right; the coast is clear. Room 503 is homeroom. As I walk up the stairs, I pay attention to everything around me. "There is not going to be a freshman beat down here," I repeated to myself.

*Oh, no,* I thought as two students walked up to me.

"Are you a freshman?"

"No," I swiftly replied, "I'm a sophomore. I came from another school."

"Oh, okay," they replied.

*What a relief. They bought it,* I thought as I sighed. I had never been happier that I looked older than I really was. I later realized that the threat of a beat down was all a scam to keep the freshmen in their place.

***Alexis Polanco** is a high school graduate in Boston and a proud writer and poet who was recently published in the 826 Boston book* Small Things Can Grow Tall. *He hails from the Dominican Republic, which he hopes to visit soon. Alexis will attend college at the Universal Technical Institute for automotive studies, and plans to study aviation as well.*

# High School in My Shoes

Justin "Fuzz" Dennis, age 19
Ann Arbor

## NINTH GRADE: BAD END TO A GOOD YEAR

There I am, sitting in my fifth-period class. I'm doing the usual, which is playing solitaire in the back of the class and ignoring my biology teacher while he talks about the phases of mitosis. While I'm trying to figure out where to place the three of clubs, my teacher tells me I'm needed in the office. My first thought is that my counselor wants to yell at me for not doing my work in biology. That's usually the only reason why I get called down to the office. I pack up my things and head out the door and downstairs to the ninth-grade class office.

As I walk in, the secretary tells me that my mom is on the phone. I pick up the phone. My mom tells me that we were evicted from our house. My eyes widen, and my heart drops to my feet. I can't come up with any words to say. In that moment my throat is dry, my head is spinning, my heart is pounding, and my stomach is queasy. All I can think about is what my family and I are going to do for shelter. I don't know where any of us are going to go. I don't know if I will be strong enough to get through this situation. My whole world is crumbling before my eyes. I can't do anything but stand here with a depressed expression on my face, the phone still in my hand.

I can't believe that this is happening to me. I've seen things like this happen to people on TV, but I never expected something like this to happen to me. Whenever you see someone in a situation like this, you don't exactly consider what you would do if you were to go through it. That's precisely what happens to me that day. I don't know what to do. I don't know where to go from here. All I know is that my life is never going to be the same again.

I snap back to reality when my mom starts to speak again. She tells me that a cab is going to pick me up and take me to what is no longer my home to pack all of our belongings. I slam the phone on the hook and fight back the tears. Once I leave the office, I see the cab has already arrived. Throughout the drive I can't get my thoughts straight. Nothing makes sense to me anymore. Everything that I once believed in has gone out the window. I realize that the only person I have in this world now is myself. It's like the game of solitaire that I was playing in class. In solitaire, you are by yourself and can only depend on yourself. Depending on how the cards play, you win or lose. Today, the cards didn't play well for my family and me, and we lost the game.

Minutes later, we pull up outside the complex where I had lived. Lined along the curb is everything that my family and I own. I see my brothers, Corey and Marcus, placing boxes, bags full of our clothes, and our televisions in a U-Haul truck. I see Marcus's girlfriend, Luarynn, helping out with the boxes. I also see my cousin Josh and a random guy I've never met before putting our tables, dressers, and furniture in the truck as well. Then I see my mom trying to put as much stuff as she can fit into small boxes and garbage bags. I also see our new kitten, Sparkle (who is still a baby—we've only had her for a week or two), in her cage under the nearest tree in the shade.

As I look around at all of our possessions, it hits me that I never realized how much the little things that we have mean to me. The coffee mugs that had just been washed the previous day, the canned goods that have never been opened, the books that have never been read are all things that I never cherished and took for granted. All of those things never meant so much to me as they do right now. Nothing in life is promised.

## BACK WHERE I BELONG

It's Tuesday, January 30, 2007, my first day back at Huron High School after I left for Chicago in July. As I walk into my morning earth science class, I look around the room for familiar faces. I see no one I know. I walk to the back of the class and take a seat.

As I wait patiently for the class to begin, I lay my head down on the table and reflect on the past seven months. I can remember it all so clearly. Every week, every day, every minute is branded into my memory. All of what I've been through in the past seven months is finally at an end.

After being evicted, with no place to call home, and having to move into my aunt's house in Chicago, I thought I would never see Ann Arbor or my friends again. After having to attend Bowen High, where I had to go through metal detectors when entering the school, wear a blue school uniform that took away my individuality, and was forced to sit in a class where the teachers could never finish a lesson plan due to the loud students, I thought I would never get a full and proper education. After having to walk the cold streets of Chicago where my brother almost got shot, where drive-bys happened on a monthly basis, where kids were being jumped and beaten up because they attended a different school, and where drug addicts would try to mug you, I thought I would never be safe again.

But that's all over now. I'm back in the one place where I feel safe and comfortable. I can now relax and rest my head knowing that all is okay. I can smile now because I know that in a few short hours I will be reunited with all my friends during lunch. I'm happier than ever now, and nobody can take that away from me. Not God himself. This is my day, and I am going to take advantage of it.

"Good morning, class. Let's begin."

## TENTH GRADE

On the clean, white surface of my refrigerator, a certificate is posted. It's a beige piece of paper with peach-colored waves lining the inside edges. If you look close enough, you can see the perforated margin where the certificate was torn off. But there, written in the middle of the paper, are the words that are tattooed on my heart: "The poem written by Justin Christopher Dennis has been chosen of high merit for publication." Never has a small piece of paper meant so much to me. The feeling of success rages throughout my body. Although I'm blank and emotionless on the outside, on the inside I'm smiling and bursting out in joy. I'm smiling because now I know that I have what it takes to achieve my dream. I know that with my drive and determination, I can do anything. No longer am I just Corey and Marcus's little brother. No longer am I just Justin the high school student. I'm Justin the published poet, and now I have nowhere to go but up.

***Justin "Fuzz" Dennis*** *is a senior and was born and raised in Ann Arbor, Michigan. He received the nickname "Fuzz" (a reference to his hair) in sixth grade from one of his close friends. He is the youngest of three brothers. Justin likes to write short stories and poetry, hang out with friends, draw on occasion, and watch television. After high school, Justin plans to get a job and later, to attend college while still continuing with his writing.*

# Bars

## Adrienne Flowers, age 17
Ann Arbor

SIXTH GRADE

As soon as I walk in the room everybody looks down. Is it my cuffs, a scuff, or because my shoes are brown? The girl next to me asks, "Ayo! How much those hit you for?"

I say, "Around $120, $122.04."

Reply: "Oh, cool." *Tsk tsk!* School is not a shoe store.

EIGHTH GRADE

Eighth grade, eighth grade. Seems like seventh grade. Same games, but just an older arcade. I feel like I'm older. But still I'm so young, but I feel very proud of what I've become. I look around and the kids are still kids. I mean, they have so far to go. Because I feel twenty-two, and the others are twelve years old. Maybe it's just me. Because I'm eleven. Which would make me the youngest in the class.

TENTH GRADE

The halls are white bricks; the library is in the middle. There are about six huge windows that let you see into the library. The lockers are red, the floors and doors are tannish-yellow. A hall monitor walks into the hall. I'm not worried; I crack a joke. "What's up, homie? What you got this hour?"

She laughs. "Girl, where you supposed to be at?"

I say, "Here." Then ask her that back.

She says, "A hall sweep is about to take place." So I knew the fifth floor was my next space. I'm out!

Text message from Doma: *Where you at?*

Reply: *I'm on the third floor, you?*

Text message: *I'm on the fourth. I'll be down in two.*

Reply: *Naw, meet me on the fifth, man. The first bathroom on the odd side by Mr. O's room.*

Text message: *All rite, fasho, I'll see you.*

We get to the fifth. Then hear the announcements. "A hall sweep is in effect. Any students found where they are not supposed to be will be brought down to the office for referrals."

In my head I'm like, *They're not going to catch me. I'm straight on that.* So me and Doma skip, until five minutes of class are left. We walk out the bathroom and go to the third floor. It's Mr. Plow standing at the door. Walkie-talkie in his hand, his eyes on us. We play it off, but he stops both of us.

"Passes?" Now we are both looking dumb. We both get suspended—great.

### TWELFTH GRADE

Oh my God. That's all I have to say.
Twelfth grade, twelfth grade.
Every night, every day.
It's more and more . . . complicated.
It's stressful, it's continuous drama,
my wounds never mend.
I should never have taken it easy in the beginning, because
it's harder in the end.
And it's more and more . . . complicated.
I'm more and more frustrated, irritated, humiliated because
I'm not where I'm supposed to be.
In my dreams it rubs it in harder than dry lips
and Vaseline do, when it gets hard.

Whelp, I think it deserves to be my fault because
I . . . me, did the dumbest things.
And that makes it more and more complicated, for me.

***Adrienne Flowers** is a high school senior in Ann Arbor, Michigan. Born and raised in Detroit, Aday (as she is known around school) developed a love for hip-hop at a young age. These days you can find her rapping at every opportunity, performing at school assemblies, and distributing several mix tapes. Upon graduation, Aday plans to continue her education while pursuing a career in music.*

# No Turning Back

Cynthia De Jesus Hernández, age 17
Los Angeles

ELEMENTARY: THIRD GRADE

My third-grade teacher was a woman who wanted us to succeed. She was the first teacher to talk to us about college. She told us what it was, and I truly believe that she wanted all of us to go. She put it bluntly: if she ever saw one of us working at McDonald's, she would throw a drink in our face. Being a small kid of only nine years, I thought this was scary, but now I see that she was trying to get us to realize that we can do more with our lives.

In order for us to learn how to multiply and to memorize our multiplication tables, our third-grade teacher had us compete against other classes. This started my competitive streak. Excitement filled the classroom when we heard that a class was coming for a multiplication contest. When the other class came, our teacher made both classes get into rows. She told us the rules: whoever answered the multiplication problem the quickest would win a point for their class, and the losing person would be eliminated from the game.

The whole game was going by quickly. Things got more tense as both classes lost people. I was still in the game; my memorization skills were working for me. As I passed each round, I was confident that I would help my class win, but my confidence faded away once I saw this other girl who was faster than me. Every time one of my classmates went up, she always beat them. She answered so fast that you barely realized what had just happened. As more of my classmates lost, I began to get nervous.

All of my classmates were out of the game, and I was the only one left. The other girl was calm, and I was nervous and fidgety. The teacher held up the flash card, and before I could blink, the girl yelled out the answer. Her classmates cheered while mine groaned in disappointment. I was stunned for a second, then disappointed, and then finally I realized it didn't matter. It was just a game, after all. Little did I know that next year I would meet that same girl and that we would become friends.

### SPELLING BEE

Every year from the second grade on, I joined the school spelling bee. I always dreamed of winning, but every year my nerves got to me, and I lost. No matter how hard I studied and how well I had the words memorized, I could never get past the first round. The spelling bee was held in the school auditorium, where there were chairs lined up for the contestants. When I entered, I couldn't stop reciting the spelling bee words in my head. *Animal. A-N-I-M-A-L. Animal. Explore. E-X-P-L-O-R-E. Explore. Syllable. S-Y-L-L-A-B-L-E. Syllable.* I kept thinking to myself, *I can do this.*

Before the spelling bee began, the judge explained the rules to the contestants. She started with the easiest words, and most of the contestants passed. I knew how to spell every word she gave them, but when my turn came up, I was a nervous wreck. The judge gave me the word *beard*, and in my head I pictured the word spelled out perfectly: *B-E-A-R-D.* I was so sure I was going to get it right, but as I was spelling it correctly in my head, my mouth was saying something completely different. I responded out loud: "Beard. B-E-E-R-D. Beard."

It wasn't until I yelled out the second *E* that I realized my mistake, but there was no turning back. Even though I knew that I spelled it wrong, it was still a shock to me that I lost. As soon as I left the stage and sat down with the rest of the audience, I felt all of my nerves go away. I was glad that I wasn't feeling sick any more, and after the spelling bee finished I was all right with losing. I just reminded myself that I had another year to try out.

### MIDDLE SCHOOL: I-SEARCH

In the eighth grade, I was told that I was expected to write a year-long research paper; it was a requirement for graduating middle school students who were in Honors English. The research paper was called the "I-search" because the students got to pick their topics. I chose to research plastic surgery. I wanted to inform myself about the procedures, and I thought it might be a career choice for me. I also had heard that more and more teens were getting plastic surgery, and I wanted to show my classmates its dangers.

First semester, I read fiction that either involved plastic surgery or people changing their personal looks. The more I researched, the more I was interested in how much people could change their appearance. At the beginning of the second semester, my teacher taught us how to write business letters and how to conduct interviews. I sent letters out to a few plastic surgeons. I received replies to some of my letters, but they were just form letters and plastic surgery pamphlets. No one responded to my questions. After that, I interviewed two people who had had plastic surgery. One woman had gotten breast implants, and the other had had liposuction. I learned that plastic surgery isn't all that glamorous, and that there are consequences, including death, if you don't follow the strict post-op rules or if you get plastic surgery on the black market. I also learned that plastic surgery wasn't one of my top career choices: I wanted to pursue other options.

When the I-search first began, my teacher had us do weekly reports on our projects. Every time we did this, I always waited until the last minute to do them. While doing this project I experienced my first late, late nights, and learned that I'm a big procrastinator. I also learned that, although I procrastinate, I tend to concentrate on what I am doing. When the end of the first semester came, my teacher told us that we needed to complete half of our research paper and turn it in. I wrote my paper and turned in a thirty-page report. I was shocked at how thick it was when I turned it in.

As the end of the school year came, I had to finish up and prepare a big folder with my research paper, the letters I sent, and the notes I took. On the day before the due date, I revised my research paper and began writing the notes that I was supposed to have been writing throughout the whole year. Around four in the morning, I grew tired. I had written a huge pile of notes, and I stopped there. When I entered the classroom the next day, I turned in my folder with its sixty-page research paper and waited for my grade. I got full credit, and, for the first time, I was really proud of the work I had done.

### HIGH SCHOOL: INSPIRATION

When musicians are asked who their inspiration is, they always mention other singers or bands that they have listened to since they were little. Something that those other musicians did made them realize that they wanted to be in the music industry. The same thing has happened to me, but instead, I was inspired by a teacher.

My ninth-grade teacher had us read a novel about a girl who was sold into the sex trade in India. While we read the book, our teacher told us even more information about brothels. She told us that she knew so much because she had participated in raids to free child sex slaves. She also told us how the children need psychological help to overcome their traumas.

It was then that I realized that if I ever became a psychologist, I wanted to help children, especially those who have gone through the same situations as the girl in the novel. While I had always thought about the possibility of becoming a psychologist, I had never determined that for sure. It was then that I realized what one of my career choices would be once I graduated. Although my ninth-grade teacher probably told us her experiences to help us understand the novel better and to make us realize that places like that exist, she may not have realized that she also inspired us to help people.

TRIGONOMETRY TEACHER

I'm in the eleventh grade at my high school now, and I have met many great teachers. One of my favorite teachers this year is my trigonometry teacher, who always cares about her students' education and offers her help. She does extra tutoring in the morning, and she always has us ask her about homework problems that we do not understand.

I think my trigonometry teacher is unique because she cares about how her students feel in class. She has us create portfolios in which every one of us has the right to critique her teaching methods and say whether they're helping or not. She also tries to keep her students in a happy mood by making us laugh; she knows that if she keeps us in a good mood, we are more likely to listen in class. Whenever I ask for help in the morning, my trigonometry teacher is always willing to help. She has never looked mad about helping someone; she's always happy to help because she really wants her students to pass the class and to learn. She's one of those teachers who makes you feel glad to have her. If she wasn't my math teacher, I would probably be having a hard time.

***Cynthia De Jesus Hernández*** *was born in 1992. She's a big fan of the Harry Potter series. She read the last book in fifteen hours, including sleep and break times. She is also a Stephen King fan.*

# A New Stage

Michael Liu, age 17
Ann Arbor

### A NEW STAGE

The plane flew through the darkness, crossed half of the world, carrying my dreams and soul across the Pacific Ocean. I would never know whether this was a good choice, but I had already begun my chase for the new, challenging life. I said good-bye to everything in Shanghai. Life is just like a feather in the wind, with nobody able to control what our destiny will be. Having a sense of nostalgia and a sense of hope—wishing for no regrets—I started my new journey in a city called Ann Arbor, a place fated to be my second hometown.

### MARCH

Despite the twelve-hour time difference and fourteen-hour flight, I was so eager to find out what the strongest country looked like. All the way from the Detroit Metro Airport to Ann Arbor, I tried my best to observe every detail of the new place. The clear blue sky of early springtime was like a large piece of silk. Green was hidden behind the withered yellow but still showed the energy of new life. Cars were passing through like steeds, and the speed told me what a nation on wheels was like. Forty minutes flew by quickly, and I finally got to Ann Arbor, a small city based around the University of Michigan. Without skyscrapers, the whole town was harmonious under the clock tower of North Campus. Squirrels used their curious eyes to welcome the newcomers. The English words and people of different skins were always telling me: *You have already stepped on to a new stage for your life.*

APRIL

I enrolled at Huron High School a mere seven days after I arrived. This year, for me, was mainly spent learning Western culture and customs. Also, a special study experience in American teaching methods attracted my attention. My new high school stood near the Huron River; the main building used its hallway to display the history of the area. Modern facilities let me enjoy the advantages of technology. To my surprise, I found many Asian American faces on the way to the main office, and I felt excited and a little bit worried, because I knew studying here would be very competitive with a group of students with black eyes and yellow skin. My counselor was a warmhearted and helpful young lady. Her smile encouraged me to pick up my English soon. Nearly all the teachers were surprised at my English level when they didn't know I had already studied English for fourteen years.

MAY

Bias, absolute bias! After the first weeks' happy time, I became shocked to learn what advanced placement classes here were like. During the second hour of my physical science AP class, I encountered dozens of academic words like *stratosphere*, *granite*, and *marble*, which I had never seen in English before. I didn't remember how, but nearly all the students and teachers in China all had one idea—that studying in the United States was easy and happy. That's the reason many parents wanted to send their kids here, especially the ones with poor scores. Now this rumor seemed so superficial to me. Yes, it seemed that the American students had lower education levels, but we did not know it was just for early education. As soon as all students get to high school, they face all the lessons that give them access to what they might choose as their future jobs. Each course offers a great number of new concepts and knowledge, and is taught in a short period of time. Furthermore, the advanced placement lessons hold twice as much information as ordinary ones. The speed and the homework make newcomers really struggle. How can we say studying here is without pressure and stress? Maybe what my father once said was right: to be an excellent student anywhere is always a challenge that requires time and energy. One night, I put this new experience on my Facebook page to share with all my friends who thought I had escaped the highest level of education.

***Michael Liu*** *is a high school junior in Ann Arbor, Michigan. He left Shanghai, China, for America in March 2009. As a foreign student who enjoys both Eastern and Western culture, he got used to the life here very quickly. His greatest interest is reading books, even though all the books he reads in English class are tragedies.*

# The Beautiful Spotlight

## Tracy Arteaga, age 18
Boston

THIRD GRADE: THE BEAUTIFUL SPOTLIGHT
Boston, Massachusetts

I had grown a few inches and gained a few more pounds since first grade. The only thing that stayed the same was that I kept getting into trouble. One Monday, I remember standing in line with my class. We were preparing to recite the Pledge of Allegiance, and the principal chose me to come up to the stand and help them say it.

There were over a hundred students and teachers; the whole school was there. At the beginning, the crowd was loud, but as I started talking, all the teachers and students, from kindergarteners to fifth grades became so quiet that I could have heard a feather fall to the ground. It was so amazing; I felt like I had the attention of all the people for the first time in my life. After that day, I felt so special because I had been there for three years and I hadn't led the pledge once before that day. Some kids had recited it three times in one year, but not me. I just didn't seem to fit in.

This was an incredible thing I had done. I saw the world from a different point of view, and I wanted to be involved more with school. I felt like I could do what other people did, without being left out. I learned that if you really want something, it doesn't matter whether you're rich or poor, ugly or pretty; you could make anything happen. It's all about what you want and putting effort into it. All I needed was some extra help and support from my teachers, which I realized I should have taken advantage of sooner.

### SIXTH GRADE: GRACIAS MAMA

Tijuana, Mexico

In sixth grade I was living in Mexico, where you graduate from elementary school after sixth grade, unlike in the United States, where you go to middle school after the fifth grade. That year, I would say, was my best so far.

I was the most popular girl in school, and I was captain of the cheerleading team. When I graduated from sixth grade I was recognized for achievement, attendance, and extra work that I had done in and out of school.

I remember that day so well. My mom made me the most beautiful dress in the whole school. It was pink with a big rose on my right hip. I was wearing high heels, and my hair was done in small curls. I was like a princess from a beautiful story. I was also happy because I had all my family with me, and, most important, my mother. My family took many pictures of me and even paid professional photographers to take my picture. My mom was in charge of the ceremony for my graduation. In the excitement of the day I forgot to thank my mother for coordinating the graduation ceremony. Even now, I still regret not thanking her, because it meant a lot to me that she was finally involved in my school and education.

***Tracy Arteaga** is a graduate of the English High School in Boston. Her proudest moment as a child was reciting the Pledge of Allegiance in front of her entire elementary school, a moment that is memorialized in this book. She plays soccer at her high school and hopes to play professionally someday. She also aspires to study cosmetology and open her own hair salon.*

# Rediscovering Me

Arthur Rishaud Thomas, age 18
Boston

## FIRST GRADE: REDISCOVERING ME

First grade, my teacher was Ms. Rudder, and I valued her presence in the classroom because I could relate to her: she was an African American woman who had grown up in the same environment that I lived in, and she liked onion and garlic chips. She treated me like one of her own children. She was pretty stern with us, like a parent would be. Our assignment every day was to copy a statement off the board, and we had to do it even around Christmas time. One of the other students and I were not done, and we didn't get our presents until finished. One time I accidentally called Ms. Rudder "Ma." She responded, "I ain't your mother!"

Academically, she challenged us, and I remember I had trouble when it came to these moments. One time, she gave us these little red books, and she told us to write the number 10 on them. Inside the books, she asked us to write down all the ways to get to 10, and I will never forget that moment when I realized my thinking was pretty unique. I was the only one who couldn't fathom any other answers besides 5 + 5 = 10. The class just moved on, so I never got a response from the teacher. Another time we were doing an assignment with pictures that we had to describe with words. There was this picture showing a pair of feet, and all the kids were putting "foot" under it, and I was the only one who put "feet." I showed it to the teacher, and she had everyone change their answers to match mine. This was a different experience for me, and it helped me realize that when I do have answers for teachers, I am not very confident about my own ideas and what I know.

### SECOND GRADE: MESSING AROUND

We had this Spanish teacher named Ms. Vidal, and when I got an A– on the Spanish test, she was so happy. She hugged and kissed me, and I thought that was funny. It happened to be the highest score in the class. I didn't know what the big deal was—I just knew enough Spanish to know if someone was badmouthing me.

At home, I wasn't in an environment where my books were ready to be pulled out and read; I was faithfully dedicated to video games and Nickelodeon. This worsened my work ethic and it messed up my performance in school. My weak work ethic carried on to second grade and was exposed through the little notebooks we had to write in for about twenty minutes every day. By the middle of the year, there were kids with nearly a hundred notebooks, and I had thirteen. Most of my stories in these books were about video games and cartoons and pizza. Everyone else had written stuff about their families or talents and hobbies they took up, when I had written things that didn't even make sense.

### FOURTH GRADE: PRICELESS BEHAVIOR

We had fun in the fourth grade—which, some would say, interrupted the class. We were just practicing things we were taught: if we yelled out and made funny noises, we were making sure we understood onomatopoeia. If we shouted curse words, we thought we were using interjections to express our strong emotions. We hosted Socratic seminars on topics such as: Who is the best rapper? Which is the best soda, Coke or Pepsi? And who was wife material, Christina or Britney? We even practiced team-building activities. If my friend would rap, then I would make the beat. I didn't understand then and I still don't understand why this stuff is frowned upon in the classroom.

***Arthur Rishaud Thomas** is a high school senior in Boston. He is proud to be so close to finishing high school and considers himself a work in progress. Given unlimited plane vouchers, Arthur would travel to Brazil, where there are many people of color; Russia; Japan; or India, where* Slumdog Millionaire *was filmed. He hopes to be happy as a high school graduate and to be associated with something great in his adulthood. He vows never to assimilate.*

# Dead Poets Society

## Jamel Richardson, age 17

Boston

SECOND GRADE: JASMINE DIAZ

Providence, Rhode Island

Jasmine Diaz. She had blond hair, wore ugly Champion shoes, and had a gap between her teeth. But she smelled like candy—her breath always smelled like peppermint—so if you were talking to her with your eyes closed, she was the perfect girl. The kids always treated her like she was a monster. They called her Smelly Diaz.

"Hi, my name is Jasmine. What's your name?" she asked curiously.

"Jamel Jaquon Richardson," I replied.

"You're cute," she said, with this weird smile that showed all her teeth.

I looked at her, confused, wondering why she was talking to me.

THIRD GRADE: CRYBABY

Providence, Rhode Island

Ricky D. That's what all the kids called him. He was my height, which was pretty tall for our age. For some reason, he always picked on me. One thing my mom told me was "If someone hits you, hit him back," but Ricky D. never hit me. He just always talked about me.

"You have a huge head, man; it's like a giant's," he said, laughing.

"Leave me alone," I said, hoping he would stop.

"What? You going to cry, crybaby?"

I balled my hand into a fist and just swung.

EIGHTH GRADE: THE HERO

Providence, Rhode Island

Luis Santana was the tallest little person I had seen in my life. He had a brush cut and always wore a pair of Jordans, but people couldn't get past his height.

"Hey, jumbo shrimp," a kid with blond hair and a white shirt said to Luis. Luis didn't answer. "What, you mad? Are you going to head-butt me in my nuts?" the blond-haired kid said.

I opened my milk and threw it at the blond-headed kid, and then everyone started to throw food.

"Thanks, man," Luis said, looking up at me.

"Anytime," I said, feeling good about myself. I wish that feeling had lasted longer.

"What were you thinking?" the principal asked.

NINTH GRADE: DEAD POETS SOCIETY

Florida

*Dead Poets Society* is a movie that affects teachers. Why, I don't know. You can tell which teachers had watched it and which hadn't. My history teacher in Florida, Mr. Rellya, had watched the movie.

"Today we're going to learn about Machiavelli. Everyone knows Tupac, right?" Mr. Rellya said excitedly.

"Yeah," the whole class said at once.

"Well, even Tupac read. That's how he got his name: Makaveli," he said. "Machiavelli believed the only way to defeat your enemies is to fake your death."

The whole class had their eyes focused on the teacher, waiting for more information.

It was painfully obvious that my seventh-grade history teacher had never seen *Dead Poets Society*. He was supposed to teach us history. I guess he got the job because he looked the part, with his glasses and suit, but he didn't live up to his appearance. He sat at his desk staring at his computer screen most of the period. By the end of the year, the only name he knew in our class was Dell. He gave us bookwork, but he didn't grade it. The only way you could fail was if you never came to class or got in between him and his beloved Dell.

I prefer teachers who have seen the movie to ones who haven't.

***Jamel Richardson** is a high school senior and has lived in Boston, Rhode Island, and Florida. He values happiness and wealth, and hopes one day to support himself and his family doing something he loves.*

# 3

# "Going for Broke"

"So any citizen of this country who figures himself as responsible—and particularly those of you who deal with the minds and hearts of young people—must be prepared to 'go for broke.' "—James Baldwin

In 1963, James Baldwin delivered the above statement in a speech aimed at educators. Forty years later, in 2003, a teacher named Kathleen Large asked her students at Leadership High School to respond to these provocative words. After the first drafts were complete, 826 Valencia partnered with Kathleen Large and her eleventh-grade English classes to create a book called *Talking Back: What Students Know About Teaching.*

*What does it mean to "go for broke?" What does it mean to be a student in the U.S. education system?* These are just some of the questions Leadership High School students tried to answer in seventy-one insightful essays that talk honestly about their experiences in school, giving important and authentic advice to educators everywhere. *Talking Back* was not just a way for these students to voice their opinions but also was one of the first books to highlight youth talking about the day-to-day failings and triumphs of the U.S. education system. That book was the inspiration for this one.

Almost eight years later, 826 National has asked students in all eight of our chapter cities to write about their experiences in school. In this chapter, middle and high school students once again let us know what "going for broke" means to them. Hopefully their insights will inspire adults to "go for broke" as we engage students more deeply and help them reach their potential.

# Silence Is Not Always Golden

Dani Navarre, age 18
Seattle

A shiver runs down the back of my spine, and my daydreams are suddenly wrenched away. As my head snaps up, the feeling of thirty pairs of eyes meet my gaze. A slight twinge of panic pains my chest as the room suddenly becomes uncomfortably warm, and I reluctantly raise my eyes toward the authority figure standing before me. The sleepy thoughts wane as my mind is thrown into overdrive as it must now overcome the challenge, the ordeal, of being unexpectedly called upon. Not only do I try to somehow remember the question that was asked, but I must also in some way think of a suitable answer before the growing silence becomes excruciatingly awkward.

The whiteboard is covered in Spanish phrases as thirty pencils furiously write—nothing but a blur of yellow and the sound of lead against paper. No one notices as the teacher moves toward the front of the classroom, but every eye turns toward me when a question is posed. In the piñata-adorned room, the Señora stands inquisitively and repeats, "Dani, what is the present subjunctive tense?" With the wheels of my mind turning and the answer on the tip of my tongue, the feeling of failure cannot help but overcome me. I manage to squeak "No sé," and then shrink back into my desk, wishing for the ability to disappear. Alas, my superpower is not granted, but my participation points magically shrink.

Spanish III is not the only confrontation I meet daily; this ongoing battle takes place every time I step into a classroom. Although there is insecurity, this is an improvement from my younger years, when I would tremble when asked to speak to the class. However, my progress is far from over.

Every student at any school will at one time or another deal with the fright of being put on the spot by their teacher. Some meet this opportunity with grace, by reciting the precise response to the question. Others, like myself, experience stage fright. We can barely squeak out an audible answer before turning our wide eyes to stare at our desks or simply state the timeless reply "I don't know." Perhaps our lack of response or an intelligent answer makes us appear unprepared, slow, or lazy. This, however, may not be the case for an introverted person such as myself. I know that I know the answer. Convincing the teacher that I can perform takes a little more effort. Although it is a rare occasion that I voluntarily give a response, when I do muster up the courage I try to respond sincerely, yet in my mind my response lacks luster.

Some are born to be great debaters, challenging every opinion with their own. Others prefer sitting at the back of the room praying and hoping not to meet the teacher's daunting glances, hunting for a victim. I can recite a memorized speech with such ease that I am often told that I could be an anchorwoman. On the occasions that I am called upon randomly, however, I am a deer in headlights. It is not that I do not know the answer, but that I am caught off guard by the question. It is difficult to process such information on the spot and be expected to generate an answer in a matter of moments. It also does not help to have anxiety about facing the consequences of answering incorrectly—embarrassment and the feeling of idiocy.

Public humiliation is one of the many fears with which students commonly deal. Other times, we fail to answer the question at all. We respond in silence, only to turn to a friend and say "I knew it" after the answer has been stated. Saying "I don't know" feels like admitting defeat, like a public declaration of stupidity. No matter how out of proportion this reaction may seem for such a simple mistake, it can greatly hurt a student.

Teachers, I ask you, in any way that you can, not to judge that student at the back of the room who barely speaks. I ask you to help and understand them, to put yourself in that desk. Find a way to create an environment that will bring out the shyer students in the classroom. Perhaps smaller, more intimate group discussions could be utilized in order to debate a response to a question and then present it. As well as preparing the student, it would eliminate the element of surprise. A list of questions or key terms could be given out the night before, with students expected to discuss them the next day in class. Also, at the beginning of class, teachers could discuss the topic of study for the day and give specific questions to an individual student with a set amount of time in which to prepare an answer. This would allow the student adequate time to process the question, look through his or her notes, and be able to think of an appropriate answer.

Moreover, I urge teachers to focus more on the process of explanation and the ways in which a student arrives at an answer, rather than whether or not he or she is correct. Create an interpersonal place where students feel safe to express their ideas. School could be a place where students are not chastised for making a mistake, but rather receive praise for giving their best effort.

The student in the back has as much of a voice as the classmate who is constantly talking. Empower that student to reach and grow, and let that voice breach the silence. Before he or she fades into the background, let him or her know that they can and will be heard. Everyone has a voice, and everyone should be able to assert that right without fear of judgment.

**Dani Navarre** *was born in Kirkland, Washington, in 1992 and continues to reside there. She enjoys photography, writing, and reading. Dani loves working with her school's National Honor Society, Beta Club, and International Club, as well as volunteering at the Kirkland Municipal Court. She is a member of Summer Search, whose staff and mentors gave her the strength to reach beyond her wildest dreams. She plans to attend college and go into the field of education.*

# We Have Already Gone Broke

Gabriela June Tully Claymore, age 17
San Francisco

I sat in front of the television tonight as Barack Obama gave his first State of the Union address, watching Nancy Pelosi repeatedly tousle her hair, when the President declared, "The best antipoverty program around is a world-class education." I have found myself disappointed by some of the president's campaign promises over the past year, but this single statement truly emphasized why an educator must "go for broke" in the United States and the esteem the government is supposed to have for our public education system. But "going for broke" does not have metaphorical connotations today in relation to public education; it translates quite literally that, in order to receive a proper and fulfilling education, one must go broke. As a high school junior who has attended public school in San Francisco for twelve years, I have witnessed the dismantling of the California public education system, one budget cut at a time. The future of education in this country no longer resides in the dedicated and capable hands of public-school teachers, but in the government's back pocket.

This is not to say that the government does not care about education, but it is apparent that over the years, amid so many international and economic issues, education has become less of a priority for both the federal and state governments. In California, when there is a budget crisis (which there has been for as long as

I can remember), the first cuts always come from the schools, which theoretically should be the last place the state government should deprive of funding. In the eighth grade, my Spanish language arts teacher personally purchased copies of the novel *La Vida Loca* by Luis Rodriguez in order to complete a dwindling class set. The book, an autobiographical account of the author's life as an adolescent gangster living in Los Angeles, was riveting. It was the most honest novel I had ever read, and for some other students it was a reflection of the brutality they had witnessed in their own lives and neighborhoods. A parent deemed the book inappropriate, saying it was too graphic, too mature, for middle school kids, and the school decided to abandon teaching it in the upcoming year. Every copy, including the thick paperbacks my teacher bought, was returned to the middle-school library once we had finished reading the novel.

Teachers often shoulder the cost of classroom supplements and supplies by paying for the resources that, in a public school, should be guaranteed. I hear the underpaid, overworked public-school educator's mantra repeated over the years: "I paid for these out of my own pocket—please treat them with respect." I told that teacher, a week before my graduation from eighth grade, that she should not stop teaching the book and to forget all of the controversy surrounding her choice of decent adolescent literature. She smiled and told me that although she would not be able to assign it in class, the books would continue to be available to any incoming students who were interested. My language arts teacher understood that though her students were still young, we were capable of understanding concepts and emotions that some adults believed were too mature for fourteen-year-olds, and she advocated for our exposure to unorthodox literature.

It is possible that the government's failure to prioritize education is due to the development of and heavy reliance on standardization. While my report card might have said that I had an aptitude for spelling and a whimsical artistic sensibility, instead I was labeled "proficient" as early as the second grade. Schools in San Francisco are segregated into two categories: the high scoring and the low scoring. I went to a low-performing middle school, and in the seventh grade the scores were so poor that teachers' jobs were threatened because they did not "teach to the test." In seventh grade, my frazzled and indignant social studies teacher taught government-approved lessons while a state-employed woman observed her teaching methods, quietly taking notes in the back of the classroom. We knew she was an intruder; adult legs are too long to fit under those battered wooden desks. Even the rowdy students behaved themselves in the presence of these strangers, acting interested in the lessons, quietly resting their heads on top of three-ring binders, or staring blankly at that spot in the ceiling where the tiles did not line up right. It became important that our teacher look good in front of these people who infiltrated our classrooms constantly, harassing our teachers and sentencing us to hours of boredom. I happened to have some of the most inspired and dedicated teachers during those three grueling adolescent years of middle school. These teachers exemplified the idea that in order to be successful, an educator must love working with and guiding young people, inspiring them to become creative, intelligent adults.

Many of these difficulties inspire apathy throughout communities, leading people—especially adolescents and children—to believe that they do not deserve more from a public school system. This mind-set encourages parents to seek out a better education for their children in private institutions where the teaching is always adequate and resources plentiful, but for a price. It is unreasonable to believe that a public school should have the same resources as a private one, but there are fundamental ideals that socially divide public school and private school students. Often public high school students sneer at kids who attend private schools because we see the public education system as a prelude to living in an unjust world. This bigotry is objectionable, because the United States is supposedly the home of equal opportunity and the American dream, but realistically it reflects our high school idea that public school hardens kids and serves them up for a working-class future.

Nancy Pelosi is smiling and nodding now, like a bobblehead on the dashboard of someone's decrepit sedan on the highway. The Democrats are overwhelmed with pride and stand, for the umpteenth time, to applaud the forty-fourth president, and I realize that I cannot hold George W. Bush responsible anymore. The lack of funding for public schools cannot be blamed on individuals, though it is unclear where the spending on our country's education system went. The continuous budget cuts that public school students consider normal cannot possibly be just an unfortunate default in the government's spending system. San Francisco's public school budget has fallen $13 million short this year, and no amount of fund-raising will be able to assist programs that schools will be forced to cut entirely. I could blame corrupt politicians and ignorant celebrity-governors, but the truth is, public education in the United States has not been prioritized in years. It comes after bailing out corporations and fighting insurgents far from home.

The Democrats are standing now, held by invisible strings, slapping their palms together. As the president steps down and the house erupts in cheers, he leaves me wondering how we, as students and as educators, can unearth that "world-class education" that is buried somewhere far from the American dream.

***Gabriela June Tully Claymore** is a high school junior with a focus in visual arts. She loves going to the beach near her house, traipsing around San Francisco with her friends, and visiting her extended family. Gabriela hopes to continue making art in her future and plans to go to college in 2011.*

# A Lesson for Teachers

## Cesar Franco, age 21

Los Angeles

Most of my battles have been with people who were supposed to help me. People think school should be a positive environment, but that's not always the case. Some people experience joy going to school, and others experience frustration because of the way they're treated. My peers and I experienced the fear and frustration that come along with having to keep quiet about our needs. For example, there are people who tell me I shouldn't care about learning because I'm legally blind, or I shouldn't want the same things as other people because I have a disability. I am talking about my aides, peers, and teachers.

I had an elementary school teacher tell me I was too hyper to learn, and that I should tell my parents to put me on medication. Another teacher wouldn't enlarge my material and said, "You can't read anyways, so what's the point?" This made me feel mad and depressed. They pulled me apart and put me down. My teacher insulted me and wouldn't bother giving me any time, support, or care.

I tried to go from a special day class to a regular class, but I had difficulty seeing the board. The general education class had a more challenging curriculum, and it was very frustrating because the other students started to laugh at me. Sometimes the students would call me names when I asked for assistance. They would also bully the special education students, in and out of the classroom. I asked the teacher for help, but she denied my request. She told me she did not have time for me because I was a special education student and couldn't understand the material. She made me feel unimportant. The teacher did not have the patience to work with students of mixed disabilities. I think all teachers should be trained to work with diverse learners.

My first two years at Marshall High School were horrible. I had a VI (visually impaired) teacher who was himself totally blind. He wouldn't provide me with an itinerant teacher (someone who handles individual cases in many different schools). He said I didn't need it because I was in the VI program. I was given only one elective class per semester; he said I could not succeed in a regular class. He always told me that I couldn't understand his material and that he was going to put me in a class for mentally retarded kids. He kept calling me "MR," but it wasn't true.

But then he really did it! He actually spoke to my parents about putting me in what he thought was a class for the mentally retarded! Fortunately, this "MR" class turned out to be a special day class with other students of mixed disabilities, including another VI student. In this class, I had a chance to take elective classes and get all the VI materials I needed. For the first time in my life, I am receiving itinerant services (three hours each week, supposedly to make up for lost time). I even have my own Braille machine now, and I recently discovered that learning to read and write in Braille makes a big improvement in my writing with regular print. I feel like I survived the criticism, torture, anger, and abuse to succeed. I feel proud of myself now and strong enough to help others make it through the rough times like I did.

Most teachers learn from their mistakes by improving the way they treat their students in the future. Not all of my teachers were bad; if they were, I would have given up by now. In middle school, I had a regular math teacher named Mr. De Motto. He gave me lots of confidence not just in math, but in everything. He taught me that I could learn as well as other students if I tried harder. He was the first teacher who made me feel I could make it to high school and even college.

I have learned I can deal with any challenges I have in class, no matter what the teacher is telling me. Special education students need to be given equal opportunities in education and not to be judged by the way they look or by their invisible challenges. My goal is to become a special education teacher so that I can implement these lessons.

***Cesar Franco** likes to go to school and be a responsible student with his schoolwork. His favorite color is blue. He likes to read books every day. The girls drive him crazy at school because he is very handsome and nice. He and his family like to go to the beach and theme parks. He is very helpful at school with everybody.*

# The Story of My Life

Saif Ghanem, age 17
Ann Arbor

Seventh grade in Iraq was the year that changed my whole life. I grew from a kid to a young man who knew what he wanted and could take care of himself. I have some good memories and some bad ones from this grade. A good memory was when the teacher didn't come to class or was late, so we left class and played soccer. I met a lot of friends and had so much fun with them. A bad memory was when we were at lunch, playing soccer in a large field, and we heard some loud sounds coming near us and getting louder and louder. In one second a bomb fell on the side of the field and a big black cloud of smoke filled the whole field. We all started running as fast as we could. People started screaming; it was a scary moment because we thought another bomb was going to fall on us. I won't forget that moment for the rest of my life. I thought I was going to die. Thank God no one got hurt and we returned home safely. But even with all these sad memories I still learned a lot in the school and became more educated. I learned more about life and how to get the best from it.

In eighth grade my family moved to Jordan, and I had the craziest year of my life. I went from the good guy to the troublemaker. My friends and I got in a lot of trouble, a lot of fights. It was so insane that the school didn't know what to do with us. In the same year we had four math teachers, three English teachers, three history teachers, two science teachers, and two Arabic teachers. Each teacher stayed with us for a week or a month, but then he couldn't continue because we were so bad. They hit us with sticks, kicked us out of class, and took points from us. But nothing worked. Our class was so bad that the teachers didn't want to come teach us. I don't believe I learned anything that year, so I wasted a whole year of my life for nothing.

In ninth grade everything went back to normal. I went to a new, better school. The students were nice and more educated. No fights happened and there was no trouble. I started doing work, and my grades went up. Everything went great except one thing. I was the only Iraqi in that school, and at that time the relationship between Jordanians and Iraqis was bad. This was because a lot of Iraqis had come to Jordan and taken the jobs of Jordanian people, and prices went up, causing the Jordanians to worry about their economy. Jordanians also had different ideas and beliefs from me and my family. Every time someone found out that I was from Iraq they started giving me these hateful looks, implying that I didn't belong there with them. They thought that we were haters and that we were making trouble all the time.

After a while, when the other students got to know me, they actually changed their minds about Iraqi people. After they became friends with me, they found out that I was no different from them. And this was the year where I felt that I made something of my life. I changed those people's thinking, and that was a success.

In tenth grade I came to the United States and everything changed again. My life wasn't the same. Here everything is different: the people, the city, and the school. Even the houses are different. The first day of school was a long, hard day. I didn't know what to do. I got lost and spent half the time looking for the classes. I had some problems fitting in with other students because my English wasn't good. But on the second day a teacher introduced me to some students from my country who spoke my language, and they became my friends and helped me with my classes throughout the year. Without them, my school experience would have been painful and scary.

Now I have a lot of friends, and I'm doing great in my classes. My English is so much better than before. I don't know what the future holds for me, but I hope that it will be better than my past, and that for once I will stay in the same country and not lose my family and friends again.

***Saif Ghanem** is a high school junior in Ann Arbor, Michigan. He was born in Baghdad, Iraq, in 1993. He lived there for thirteen years before moving to Jordan for two years. At age fifteen, he moved to the United States, where he now lives. He enjoys, spending time with his friends, playing soccer, and swimming. He wants to go to college and study to become a dentist.*

# Home Building Class

## Travis Adkins, age 18
Ann Arbor

You know how you wake up in the morning and you don't want to go to a boring class where you have to sit and just listen to that teacher talk, and talk, and talk? It just makes you want to go to sleep because it's not fun—it's boring. If you would rather have a class that makes you think and want to get up and get going in the morning, then this is the class for you. Home Building is one of the most fun and educational classes that you could ever imagine. There's nothing better than going there in the morning and smelling the fresh-cut wood, the smoothness of the board after it's been cut, and the taste of holding new copper nails in your mouth. It makes you feel like you're starting school all over again. This is much more than a class for me; it's a new way of life.

Home Building class is amazing because, for one thing, you're not just sitting there all day. You're outside in the fresh air. And you're not there for only one hour. You're there for three, which allows you to spend more time building what you are working on. When it's time to go, I hear kids saying, "Give me one more second, I'm finishing up the L-block." We like to take our time on things because we don't want to make mistakes here. If you're taking a test you don't get a second chance, but if you make a mistake in Home Building you can fix it so you learn how to do it, hands-on. This is a class that makes you confident about how to do other things, too.

Before I could never get up in class and talk in front of everyone, but now, after taking Home Building, I like to get up and talk. I don't mind reading out loud or giving a presentation in class. Our Home Building teacher taught us how to stand up and speak loud and clear by assigning some of us to become team leaders. We had to make sure that our own crews were doing the work that needed to get done.

This is one of those classes that you can't just walk into and try to find your clique, because the class helps you become close with everyone. You have to work together to build something every day. It's that bond that you get from being with a partner for a while, and Home Building class makes that happen. It shows the hardworking side of everybody.

You also get to know teachers. They love to teach this stuff, and they are there for you every day. You are up and working with someone who is teaching you and at the same time helping you. This is a class that I do not want to give up. We call one of the teachers "Coach," but his real name is Mr. Birko. We call him "Coach" because he likes it a lot more. He's been in this type of work since he was a kid. He worked with his dad for as long as he can remember. The other teacher is Mr. Davenport, who acts like one of the kids and makes us feel like we can just be ourselves. They are both amazing teachers.

One of the most exciting things about this class is that you get to build a complete house in less than a year. There are so many things that you need to learn for this class, from building the main walls to putting in the windows and doors, from putting on the trim for the whole house to laying the hardwood floors and putting in the kitchen cabinets. Those are just a few of the things we've done. Carpentry shows you how to build stuff and makes it so much easier for you to see how to build things. So if you want a class that makes you feel like you belong somewhere and lets you work with people that you like getting to know, this is the class for you. Trust me, you won't ever regret it.

***Travis Adkins** is a senior from Ann Arbor, Michigan. He has a lot of things that he likes to do, including playing video games, being outside, and playing sports. But more than anything, he is proud that he works forty-five hours a week and still goes to school. Since he was sixteen years old, he has paid for everything himself, including car insurance, clothes, and his phone bill. In the future, he hopes to follow in his uncle's footsteps and become a police officer. He dedicates this essay to his mom, brother, and baby sister and wants to let them know how much he loves them.*

# 4

# "Help Us Help Ourselves": Essays Explaining What Schools Would Look Like if These Students Ran Them

In this chapter, we asked students to envision and write about their ideal school. What would it look like? What systems would they implement to make their school successful? What classes would they offer?

Many of the students have taken a critical look at their existing schools, most of which are in urban environments. Through this exercise, students found new and creative ways to breathe life into their imagined utopias. It will amaze you how many of the students in this chapter care about creating physically beautiful learning environments—yet even more care about being engaged by inspiring curricula.

# Buildings, Do-Nows, and Resources

Jennie Chu, age 18
San Francisco

If I ran the school, it would certainly not resemble the institution that I have grown to loathe. Being taught in an institution that was meant to be an elementary school has hampered my learning. Too often, I have sat in a classroom with forty students and watched as my teacher called the office to request more desks. With its 1970s decor and textbooks dating back to the 1990s, it is no wonder why I am relieved to graduate. I have sat on my brittle desk, unable to learn due to inefficient time management; I have been knocked into the lockers during passing periods and have been rejected from advanced classes due to the lack of teachers, interest, and funds. My high school experience has definitely not been favorable.

If I ran the school, it would definitely be a place where students can find a haven. The transformation of my current school would start with its architecture. Instead of resembling an asylum, I would remodel my current school to have multiple buildings or "wings." One of these buildings would be specifically for students to express their creativity through art inside and outside the building's walls. One of the most important things I learned in high school is that assigning projects that let students express their creativity is a better way to enrich their minds than simply assigning textbook work. The interior of my school would be painted with tints and shades of blue to foster calmness among students. There is something about the color blue that makes a person calm. Students cannot study when chaos is around the corner. I am proposing a method that will enhance the students' learning capabilities without them feeling forced—the colors and arts will be their motivational force.

If I ran the school, not a single minute of class time would be wasted. Two-thirds of my senior year courses required us to do a "Do-Now" at the beginning of class. These Do-Nows are supposed to introduce the lesson plan by asking a few questions based on the specified topic. But sometimes the total time that it takes to fully complete a Do-Now is around forty minutes. Yes, they can develop into interesting discussions, but more than likely they are a waste of time. These introductions are sometimes used as fillers in a course schedule. As the principal of my school, I would get rid of the infamous Do-Nows. Instead, I would hold mandatory meetings with all teachers to help schedule their lesson plans in a more efficient way.

If I ran the school, my remodeled school would not be completely different from any other school. The school I would run would incorporate all the best and effective aspects of my neighboring high schools: bigger hallways to accommodate the student body so no student will feel unsafe, better classroom equipment to ensure that students are learning current material, and more teachers to lower our class sizes. Students need a comfortable space to engage in learning, and I believe building and providing a more suitable environment will increase the chances of success.

My ideal school is a combination of borrowing aspects of effective present-day schools and introducing new ideas. Students should be able to express their creativity to provoke their learning habits. Teachers should be able to plan and organize an effective schedule so no class time is wasted. The school itself should serve its own purpose, providing a safe institution for eager students to learn. If I ran the school, I would achieve a school's purpose in a creative and effective way.

***Jennie Chu*** *was born in 1992 and is the first person in her family to attend college. Jennie's peers are the ones who inspire her the most. They are one of the most influential groups of people she has ever met. Without her friends, writing "Buildings, Do Nows, and Resources" would not have been possible.*

# New School

Gerardo Longoria, age 17
Ann Arbor

"Okay, I think it's cool enough. You can go ahead and close the window now," Mrs. Johnson says. I obediently go to the window and shut it, feeling the last bit of cold air pass through it.

To my left I can see snow falling all over the school grounds and past the thick forest in the background. Everything looks white. The trees have lost their leaves. There is no color besides gray or white. The trees and the sky look gray. It makes everything sad and depressing.

*Ring, ring!*

*Ring, ring!*

I hear a high-pitched ringing in my ears. For a second I don't understand what is happening. I only hear a very uncomfortable ringing. When I recognize its familiar sound, I realize what is going on. I have heard this ringing many times before. I have heard it so many times that I know exactly what time it rings.

The loud ringing of the school bell wakes me up, and I realize that I have fallen asleep in class. Everyone is putting their materials away and starting to leave the classroom. I get up quickly and put my books and notebooks into my backpack. I head for the door almost at a sprint, but before I can make it I hear someone calling my name. I turn around and I see Mrs. Johnson sitting at her desk, looking at me.

"I do not appreciate the fact that you are coming to my class to sleep," she tells me.

"I'm sorry, Mrs. Johnson. I had to stay up last night to do homework and to study for a test. Did I sleep through the whole hour?"

"No, you slept for a little less than ten minutes. Please don't let it happen again, okay? I want you to come to class to learn and be involved."

Moments later I'm walking out of the classroom with a feeling of guilt. I need to start getting more sleep! I have no idea how I'm going to do that when I have loads of homework every night. While I'm walking to my next hour, I think of all the possible solutions to my problem. Maybe doing homework early will do the trick. What if I have other things to do during the day? I might get a job or get into a sport. Why should I be limited to doing only my homework and sleeping? That is not a life.

As I walk through the hallway, I stop thinking about how to solve that problem, because I am faced with a different one. I am a couple of doors away from my class. The hallway is packed with more students than I can count. I push and shove through the crowd. Other students who are passing by also push me. Everyone is pushing, trying to get to his or her next class. Every student knows that there are consequences for being late, and they want to avoid those consequences.

Once I escape the current of students, I go into my next class. I quickly make my way to my assigned seat and wait for the class to quiet down so our teacher can start teaching. Just then the bell rings. Many students walk in late, talking and being extremely loud. My teacher asks them for a late pass, but instead they start arguing with him, telling him it wasn't their fault they were late.

As they walk to their seats, they don't stop talking. They make so much noise that the whole class cannot proceed. The teacher then asks them to sit down, be quiet, and to get their work out. They do not follow his instructions. They ignore him and just keep having small side conversations. As an authority figure, my teacher reminds the students that they could be written up. Some of them understand, but a few are left who want to be rebellious. "I wish you would," some say.

For the first fifteen minutes of class we don't move on because of the students who are not doing what they are supposed to be doing. Not until a student is written up and sent out of class do we finally get silence. Once we have the silence that is needed, our teacher starts talking about our assignment for the day. He tells us that we have a project coming up for which we will write three papers. I listen intently and hear him talk about possible topics. When he mentions "inventing a new school" as one of the topics, I immediately know that will be my topic. I know exactly what I'm going to write about.

### NEW SCHOOL PROJECT

If I were to start a new school, I would change a lot of things. I would first start off with the size of the school. I would want the school to be spacious. I would like to have a big media center with computers and a large area to accommodate people's studying needs. The library should be a nice, comfortable place for students to do work. I would also like to have lots of classrooms, because it would be better to have more classrooms with fewer students. Bigger classrooms with thirty-five students is a poor way to focus on students' needs. Smaller classes would make learning easier for students because teachers could focus on individual students and the issues they have with learning.

Next, I would create ways to help students focus more in class. Something that would be really helpful would be starting school later. An average teenager requires seven to nine hours of sleep to perform at his or her best. Starting school later would not only help students to focus but would also drastically reduce tardiness and would encourage students to come to school. After a long night of homework and studying there is nothing better than a long, good night's sleep. Now imagine waking up to a blaring alarm, feeling horrible, and barely being able to open your heavy eyes. It is very likely that you will not want to wake up. I can speak from personal experience and also from what my friends have told me. As teenagers, we do not pay attention to bedtimes. We go to sleep when we are tired. If it is two in the morning and we are not tired, we will not fall asleep. Therefore, I am proposing that the choice be given to students—not because we want to go to sleep late and wake up late, but because we want to get an education and focus on it; not because we want to watch TV until midnight, but because we want to do all our homework and not be too tired to do our classwork the next day.

I would focus on the actual experience within the classroom. In my opinion, that experience is the most important. A classroom is a place where a student needs to feel comfortable. It should be a safe place, free of bullying and teasing. I would stress regulation of bullying and teasing. Teasing can escalate into more dangerous situations. Those situations can cause violence or even lead to death.

I also think respect is very important. Students should respect their teachers and vice versa. If there is mutual respect, then there will be a healthy learning environment. Students would focus on classwork and pay more attention. How can mutual respect be achieved? Well, if students respect their teachers and give them the place they deserve in the classroom, then there would be no interruptions and no arguing between students and teachers. There would just be learning going on in the class. Therefore, if I were to start a new school I would make sure that respect was established, followed, and enforced. I believe that respect is a key component of a successful education.

If I were to start a new school, everyone would be given an equal opportunity to learn. They can take advantage of that opportunity or not. If they do, they will be supported. If they don't, they will be helped to understand why education is so important. Either way, my new school would benefit everyone.

***Gerardo Longoria** is a high school junior. He was born in Mexico but moved to the United States at an early age. He is energetic but quiet when he needs to be, such as in class. Gerardo enjoys playing sports, swimming, drawing, listening to music, working out, and reading. When he graduates, he plans either to attend the University of Michigan or a school in another state, his top two choices being California and Florida. After college, he plans to become a computer engineer.*

# Garden

Chris Olivares, age 14
Los Angeles

Gardeners care for their flowers while the flowers give radiant beauty to their surroundings in return. But has anyone ever wondered about the weeds in the garden? Have you looked at them and watched them struggle to survive in their small patch as the gardener eagerly tries to get rid of them? Have you watched gardeners as they tend to their favorite roses or daisies and ignore the silent pleas of the weeds, who want to flourish too? What? You're telling me you haven't noticed how the gardeners treat the weeds? That you're one of the roses and it doesn't matter to you? When you look at the weeds, do they just give you a seething look back?

The gardener is the weeds' worst enemy of all. The gardener does horrible things to them for no good reason, while you, the flower, aren't treated this way because you had more opportunities and didn't grow the way the weeds did. The gardener is deserting the weeds, denying them their education, and leading them down a desolate path. He helps the flowers who don't actually need as much help as the weeds, who are left out in the scorching sun to wither and die. Teachers are like these gardeners who tend only to their flowers and make them grow.

I stumble into this garden and see all these weeds ignored, drying up. One catches my eye. I see him slowly trying to turn into a flower, but no one is giving him the chance. I see how he's struggled, how he tries even though he's ignored. But no matter what, not a single gardener turns to him. The weeds change. They become something horrible, violent, that ruins their own lives and the lives of others around them.

I ask, "Why not tend to those?"

Not even looking up from his flowers, the gardener replies, "They're weeds. I have nothing to offer."

"Who says that?" I ask.

The gardener stops, turns to me, and says, "The world."

Is it because of their appearance? What they do or have done? Who decides all these things, and why are they automatically right?

I was never a weed, but I've observed what the weeds go through. I was just a few years younger than I am now when I started to notice all these things. I saw my friends, even a few enemies, fall back while I kept going. They were held back, or dropped out, or just stopped trying. I watched the teacher ignore them.

I try and help them as best I can. I do the teacher's job for him—not because anyone asked me to, but because I see the others struggle. They want to learn. I give them the small push that they desperately need. But I can't help them all. They fall, slowly but surely. This is not my job. I want the gardener to do it, not tend to his already over-watered flowers while the weeds struggle.

The gardener demands respect from all the plants but gets only cold shoulders from the flowers and defiance from the weeds. Will I join the weeds' rebellion? Absolutely. They each deserve a chance to learn. Will anyone above him listen to *us*? We'll make them listen whether they like it or not. My education is very important to me, and when I pass by others who are denied that education, my blood boils. I pass through the "ghetto," listening to all the gang members and how poorly they speak. I have a slight fear of them and pity for them. When they change, the teachers shrug it off and continue. Clearly, it is the teachers' fault that the students are becoming a stereotype and hurting their own community when they could have been someone else instead.

We, the students, are the future. The past generation is supposed to teach us to make the future better and not make the same mistakes that they did. What will our system be like if the "smart" are outnumbered by the "failures"? The ones who succeed can't solve all of our problems on their own. But with everyone at the same level of education, we can create a new world order. With the technology we have gained and will gain, we can make our community better than anyone has ever imagined. All of our thanks will be to our past generation, who taught us, gave us life, and helped us create a new world.

I don't know who you are. But I do know you can make a difference, whether you are an adult, a student, a teacher yourself, or just someone who found this lying on the streets and picked it up just for the heck of it. Help us create, not destroy. Create this new world that we idealize, or else ruin it and allow it to be consumed by anarchy. It's not just up to those who are higher up in the economic chain. It is up to you at the bottom, too, to climb higher and let your voices be heard so that you will join those above. Our future is in our hands. All we need are the skills from the old gardener to help us plant the new seeds.

***Christopher Olivares** is a strange teenager. He wants to become a writer when he grows up and hopes to be known for his writing, starting off with his essay in this book. He also wants to let all of you know that writing about yourself in the third person feels strange.*

# Those Horrid Blackouts

## Eli Ramírez, age 16

Los Angeles

Now for those horrid blackouts. See, at my school we don't have the best backup for when the lights go out. When winter comes, we tend to walk around in the dark a lot. I want to make sure this never happens in *my* school. It would be safe, and there would be lights. You know the feeling when you're in a dark cave, but you can see the bright light at the entrance? That's the feeling you would have here, and when the rain came down you wouldn't fear it—it would just wash away the past, letting you start fresh and clean.

You see, when I think of school I no longer think of a place where I can run away from the problems at home. I think of a place that makes me feel like I can never truly be good enough, like the problems I have will never go away. It's like a dark room with no way out. I wonder how I even got here in the first place. Why is it this way?

The world seems so different than it did when I was five. Then, the world was a fairy tale—my fairy tale, in fact. Now that I have grown, my tale has changed; it is no longer filled with monsters and pixies. Now my fairy-tale world would be filled with Skittles (it is my world, after all), and there would be no more silly fights (wars included). Learning would be fun and enjoyable, something you actually wanted to do.

Actually, unlike most kids, I loved school and learning at one time—at least until sixth grade, when teachers pushed my thoughts away and acted as if only they had the correct ones. In seventh grade, during fourth-period history, I was told that evolution was the reason why people were the way they were. I was told otherwise as a churchgoing girl: God made me as He wanted me. In *my* school, even if you said things that were different from what the teacher said, your unique thoughts would be respected. In my world, teachers would listen to your thoughts, not try to change them. Learning would be fun. Instead of telling students how to learn, a teacher would teach you in the way you learned best.

And I wouldn't be in the building like the one I'm in now, with no windows, nor any real walls to be found anywhere, just tons of students cramped in a place made for a few hundred. A classroom that holds twenty-six students would actually have twenty-six, not forty. If you were in a classroom here, it would be made just for you. There would be a room with high-tech stuff for those who love electronics, and a room with every color you could think of for those who might just need a little fun, crazy color in their lives. You could choose what you thought was best for you; if it did not work out for you, you could change and try out another room. I might be in a glass room looking out into the world, or I might be somewhere related to my learning topic. For history class, I would see not just pictures and movies; I would go explore Germany, where World War I actually took place.

Not only would you enjoy class, you would enjoy staying after school. You could join one of the clubs for art, graphic design, or acting, or make one of your own (just make sure you get your friends to join, to make it fun). I believe that what you do after school with your friends makes school a bit more fun.

No one who didn't want to be in my school would attend. No one could hurt you. People at my school would help build you up. You would be strong and know you could take the world head-on. My school could be for anyone—from someone who is shy and fears the world to someone who says, "Here I am, this is me"—because we have to learn that everyone is different. School wouldn't treat us all the same; in *my* school, you are your own person, and you learn to show this person to the world. You become free from what you must say, and you become free to say what you want to say. School will not be our cave; it should be, and will be, our place to learn about the world and ourselves.

So . . . how do you like my school?

***Eli (Elly) Ramírez*** *is a girl who wants to change the world by changing the way we learn. Someday she will, but for now high school will be the biggest change.*

# If I Ran the School . . .

Eleanor Hodgson, age 15
Washington, D.C.

The concept of running a school is pretty scary when you think about it. Hundreds of parents are trusting you not only with the safety of their child during school hours but also with the task of providing each and every pupil with the knowledge and skills to survive in the "real world." Students who criticize the way that their school is run probably don't always take into account all of the issues that the principal and the administrators have to take care of every day, and how not everything is as easy as ABC.

If I ran Woodrow Wilson High School and I were in charge of its 1,500 or so students, it would be a tall order to respond to the complaints and suggestions that pour in every day from parents and students, the subjects of which range from the hassle of the metal detectors in the morning to the quality of the bathrooms, from questions about renovation plans to snide comments concerning the worst end of the teacher spectrum. Thinking about having to solve all of those problems reminds me of specific problems that I have as a student, and some solutions that an administrator or teacher might be able to find reasonable.

The first issue that comes to mind is also the most discussed and inspires the most complaints: the metal detectors. When you arrive in front of the school at 8:30 in the morning, the fifteen minutes you have until the bell rings are not going to be spent catching up on gossip with your friends or organizing your locker shelf, but instead are to be endured inching through the painstakingly slow cluster of drowsy students pushing and shoving to make it through the single gray beeping archway that will always go off no matter how many bracelets, belts, or rings you remove before passing under it. This irritable mob is not the best mood-setter for a teenager at 8:30 on a Monday morning and puts the students in a grumpy, not-open-to-new-ideas frame of mind that lasts until the final bell rings at 3:15 and they are released back out into the fresh air—something that the interior of the school sadly lacks.

The commotion around the metal detectors every morning would be one thing if the process were entirely effective, but the system is not foolproof. There are still ways that students could get weapons and other unwanted items into the school; they just have to be clever about it. This brings up another issue around the metal detectors stationed at each of the three main entrances to the school: the airport-like security measures taken against these students create a serious lack of trust between the students and staff. If the students already know that the teachers don't trust them, then what motivation do they have to act trustworthy? In my opinion, the security machines have a negative influence on the sense of trust within the student body and give the sullen hallways the look of a prison more than of a high school. From the perspective of the principal of the school, the only apparent solution to this problem is to remove the metal detectors and give the students the opportunity to be trustworthy—although many people, parents in particular, would argue that it is too risky. But, as Dumbledore said in *Harry Potter and the Half-Blood Prince*, "I may be as woefully wrong as Humphrey Belcher, who believed the time was ripe for a cheese cauldron"—how is anyone expected to make progress without taking a couple of risks?

Another problem that I would try to solve if I ran the school is the state of the school's bathrooms and water fountains. Something as simple as cleaning up the bathrooms and providing fresh, cold water from all of the water fountains can dramatically change a student's perspective on how they want to spend their school day. The current bathrooms at my high school are more of a smelly hangout spot for hall-walkers to avoid patrolling administrators than an inviting place to relieve yourself between classes. The fifteen-minute wait for one of the five fully equipped toilet stalls (out of the eighteen or so that should be available) is an unappealing task that anyone with a full bladder must endure at the beginning of each lunch period. The only alternative is to go to the bathroom during class, which takes away from the student's learning time and adds to the number of disturbances in the hallways. If the school bathrooms were updated and transformed into cleaner places with some doors that actually locked and toilets that actually flushed, I know that I would look much more brightly upon the idea of going to school every day and focusing on a learning environment. This only reinforces the philosophy that the school must be set in a good environment where students are eager to go learn, but this is what Woodrow Wilson High School severely lacks. This problem has been recognized and is on its way to being solved with the construction of a new school building—something that I would have done too if I ran the school.

Looking at the problems that school systems face from the perspective of a principal is very different from that of a student, but gives me more insight into why my real principal sometimes does the things he does. If I were the principal, the two biggest issues that I would try to solve would be the problems with the metal detectors and with the quality of the school's learning environment. Yet I also think that students and administrators need to understand more about each others' positions. Students need to stop complaining so much, and administrators should stop being so condescending toward the students; both need to develop respect for each other and understand that "each must live in order for the other to survive."

***Eleanor Hodgson*** *is a rising high school junior. She was born in Collensville, Connecticut, but was raised in Washington, D.C., from the* *age of four. Next year she will be a third-year member of her school's rowing team. She enjoys reading, writing, biking, and spending time with friends and family. Eleanor plans on attending a college where she will be challenged by her peers and discover what career best suits her.*

# A Note from the Principal of Michelle Obama Senior High School

Kelsi Nicole Jones, age 17
Washington, D.C.

School isn't just about getting an education; it's also about working to become a well-rounded citizen of this country. Anyone can graduate from a public school with a 4.0 grade point average, but when you come from Michelle Obama Senior High School, there will be much more to you than a 4.0.

As you may have already noticed, our high school is named after Michelle Obama, who is the first black First Lady and is currently having a successful term as such. Michelle Obama may appear to appeal only to women, but the lifestyle that she lives is a perfect model for all young adults. I chose her name for my high school because of what you think of when you see it. If you just say to yourself "Michelle Obama," what comes to your mind? Can you picture success similar to Michelle's successes? I can, and I can see all of our students out in society fulfilling the goals they set out to accomplish.

We have approached the design of Michelle Obama Senior High School in two parts. Both of the designs were submitted by a panel of our faculty and students to create one magnificent building. The panel of students came up with some very high-tech designs that will make them comfortable in their learning environment. It was the students who proposed four separate schools for each grade level, to bring travel between classes down to a minimum. They also came up with the idea of a strip mall at the center of the campus, which will give students access to a library, restaurants, and other necessities before, during, and after the school day. Another useful part of our building built in accordance with student input is a relaxation room. If any students have been having a hard day due to social, academic, financial, or family issues, or are just stressed out in general, they have the option to visit the relaxation room, which has extremely comfortable furniture and other trinkets that will allow students and their brains to relax.

The panel of teachers have created interesting designs for our building as well. The major work of architecture made by the teachers is what we are calling "a perfect classroom." Each of our classrooms comes equipped with individual air conditioning and heating units in the room. The classrooms also have smart-board walls—every inch of wall is covered in a smart board—as a teaching aid (I'll save other details to show you on your tour of our school). Another teacher-driven design is our new, state-of-the-art teaching lounge. The last thing teachers added was a secret entrance to be used only by faculty.

Every square foot of our property was designed by either a teacher or a student because we believe that the learning environment should be created by those who are actively taking part in it. In addition to a wonderful inside look for our school, our outdoor campus is beautiful and expresses the colors of success.

Although the campus is a place to express yourself, the academic side of our school is rigorous. It takes focus and determination to achieve excellence in our academics. Every year, everyone is required to do a lifestyles project: a four-month project where each student simulates life in a certain career, with kids to care for and bills to pay. The only way you can pass this project is by paying your bills on time and living the lifestyle happily and well. Besides this project, there are of course your usual tests and quizzes, but you may have only up to two tests or quizzes in one academic day. To know that all of my students are learning, everyone fills out weekly assessments that ask what they learned for the week, how they learned it, and the ways that they think it could be taught better.

Michelle Obama Senior High School has set the highest standards and welcomes all those who believe that they can fulfill those standards. We stand out because of our academic strength and open, expressive campus. I hope that you now see what the true meaning of high school is, and conclude that Michelle Obama Senior High School is the perfect environment for your child.

***Kelsi Nicole Jones*** *is a high school senior in Washington, D.C. She is the second-oldest of five children. Kelsi enjoys spending time with her family, playing sports, and watching ESPN. She is very anxious and excited about attending St. John's University in the fall, where she will major in actuarial science.*

# Don't Sit

## Jake Lindsay, age 18

Seattle

Stand up. Stay on two feet throughout class. You can't be a role model from your seat. Being a role model is a teacher's responsibility, and if you don't set an example of leadership, enthusiasm, and success, nothing will inspire us to return to the classroom. Without a role model, our education is aimless. But our education starts at your feet! You must stand tall above the rest. Be energetic. Be inclusive. Be strong. Be nuts, if you have to. Don't be the teacher I had who only taught from the chair behind her desk. Don't be the teacher whose name I can't remember. Don't be "Mrs. Payday."

Mrs. Payday was the first teacher I had in high school. She taught Career Choices—a first-year requirement at South Whidbey High. Career Choices was basically an introductory finance class: the curriculum covered W-2s, W-4s, writing checks, and doing taxes. I was actually looking forward to the class; learning about technical financial forms seemed quite relevant to my success as a soon-to-be-independent adult. But by the end of the semester, I was starting to think that Mrs. Payday didn't care as much about writing checks as she did about cashing them.

In fact, I can't even remember how to write a check. But I do remember the stash of Payday bars Mrs. Payday kept in her desk. She never gave us any. She ate them while she took attendance and gave lectures from her chair. She would sometimes get up to hand out paperwork, but usually her TA would do that.

I'm not quite sure why we even had a TA; we graded ourselves in Career Choices. It was the only self-graded class at South Whidbey. Mrs. Payday would say: "How did you feel about the test material?" or "How would you rate your confidence in the subject matter?" Everyone passed the class. There was very little incentive to succeed and retain any of the material we learned. Judging by Mrs. Payday's enthusiasm for the subject, Career Choices was a useless place to invest any interest. Thus we copied each other's homework, notes, and tests. How could we be expected to care about the subject if Mrs. Payday herself didn't seem to care? Our general attitude toward the class was "Why do Career Choices when we could smoke pot or find out what it feels like to lie to a cop?"

*I'd feel a lot better about the "subject matter,"* I thought during the final self-evaluation, *if you stopped eating those Payday bars. One, it's kind of rude, and two, it makes me think that you only care about yourself, when you should really care about us. I don't mean to say you should share the Payday bars—just keep in mind that I came to class to be fed, not starved.*

I fell asleep on my desk during one of Mrs. Payday's chair lectures. I was out cold. I sat in the front row, too; I moved there hoping it would rekindle my interest in the class. Obviously, it didn't—I slept really well. At the time, I was ashamed of myself when I awoke, but I don't blame myself anymore. If Mrs. Payday could not get up from her desk, I should have been able to sleep on mine.

My friend Andrew woke me up at the end of class. To my confusion, Mrs. Payday and her TA had already left for lunch, and only two other students were lingering in the back of the classroom. Shouldn't Mrs. Payday have woken me up at some point? Yes, it was disrespectful to fall asleep, but I'd have been happier if she had thrown a tissue box at me and embarrassed me in front of the class. And if she had seen me asleep and whispered to everyone in the class not to wake me up as punishment, that would have been fine too. But it seems utterly irresponsible to leave me sound asleep in her room or trust that the other students would wake me up by the next period without knowing if they actually would. What, she couldn't have checked in as she left, to see, you know, if I were dead or something? She couldn't have woken me up before she left and given me a lecture about falling asleep in class? Wasn't I worth something to her? I didn't want to fall asleep; I wanted to learn. But she just looked so hopeless sitting in her chair. As if she had quit on us. If the leader gives up, isn't it understandable that the followers will too? I felt abandoned. I'd been doing my best to succeed in my first semester of high school, but Mrs. Payday just didn't seem to want to get out of her chair to help me out. Andrew, of all people, had the decency to rub my back to wake me up.

Andrew started using meth around that time. I remember the puncture marks in the crook of his elbow. He's still using. It's not that Mrs. Payday alone is responsible for his misdeeds, but I just wish that she would have set an example that could have steered him in a different direction, that could have gotten him out of his own chair to make some good choices. Because at some point during Career Choices, Andrew made the choice to give up on the next four years of his life. And it was easy for him to do. As easy as falling asleep in class.

***Jake Lindsay** is a youth mentor at 826 Seattle. He completed his senior year in high school through the Running Start program at Seattle Central Community College before going on to Whitman College in the fall of 2010. He lives in an old, small, elevated gray house in Wallingford, Seattle, where he can be found writing at his desk, reading on his bed, or playing guitar in an empty bedroom's closet (where the acoustics are louder and his singing voice sounds more manly). He plans to start one or more nonprofit organizations of his own.*

# Talking Back: Changing DCPS and Wilson Senior High School

Alex Neeley, age 16
Washington, D.C.

I turn on the television. The channel is CNN. A special report is being shown. The topic is "How to Fix Inner City Schools," and the schools that are being highlighted are those of the District of Columbia public school (DCPS) system. Chancellor Michelle Rhee is being interviewed about the struggle of running D.C. public schools and about the changes that she will be trying to make. She talks about closing schools and firing teachers and administrators. But Chancellor Rhee fails to mention during the interview a few changes that would really help the students. In this essay, I will discuss changes I would make if I were in charge of the D.C. public school system, particularly Wilson Senior High School.

What would I do if I controlled the school system? I think one of the biggest problems with the current school system is that the students do not have enough say in what is going on in their school. In the CNN interview, Chancellor Rhee said: "I'm not here to keep jobs for adults. I'm not here to keep people's paychecks. I am here for the children." Being one of these children, I believe that my opinion and that the opinions of my classmates are important.

For example, we the students did not get a say when some of our teachers were fired. While most of the teachers who were fired deserved to be fired, some great teachers, who did everything right and were beloved by their students, were let go. Another issue that we did not have any say in was our everyday class schedule. Each school in DCPS decides its own class schedules. At Wilson, each day starts with the same forty-five-minute class in the morning, followed by six other classes: three on one day and three on another day, for an hour and a half each. Personally, I do not like this schedule. While some students take art or gym every day in the forty-five minute class, some students, like me, are scheduled for a core class, like math and science, every day. This is a big problem. By the time you start learning something during this forty-five minute period, the class is over. Also, some students show up at 9:00 AM or later and cannot keep up with the rest of the students. If I were in charge, I would propose that students as well as teachers get a vote on this type of situation.

Another major problem I have at my school are the variations and abilities of my teachers. Some subjects, the teachers are grade-A, top-notch educators, while in other subjects the teachers are boring and make learning seem harder than it should be. This is a big problem in our school, because while you're being taught well in one subject, you're falling behind in another. Imagine going to college, where you're asked to write a paper on some topic for English class, and then you go to your math class and find out there is an exam next time you meet. Next class, you turn in your English paper and then take your math exam, and a week later you get everything back. At the top of your English essay your professor has written "A+, best piece of writing from a student I have ever read." But on your math test you get a D+. Now, this is a big problem. At first, you're thinking about what a great English teacher you had, but then you begin wishing that your math teacher was as good. If I were in charge of the school, I would begin focusing on certain subjects that I know need improvement, to make sure good teachers were running all of the classes.

While getting better teachers into the school is one thing I would do, another would be hiring more security personnel around the school. Too often, things are being stolen from their rightful owners.

A countless number of my friends have locked their stuff up in their lockers only to have them stolen anyway. I, too, am a victim of one of these thefts. Last year, I had my stuff safely locked away in the gym locker room. After PE class, I came back to find my lock had been smashed open with a lifting weight and all my belongings had been stolen. In my school, I would hire more security to watch over suspicious students and make sure that everything in the building stays calm.

One thing that I have noticed about people's things being stolen is that the same group of students commits the crimes. A select few are deciding to skip class and make trouble. These are the same kids who are struggling to stay in school and are repeating grades. If it were up to me, I would focus on these kids the most. I would hire teachers that could deal with these kinds of kids and make class more intimate for these troublemakers. I think that if you had four- or five-person classes for these students, they would get more one-on-one attention and would be able to keep up in their classes.

Changes are a big part of life. Some changes are good and some are bad. The changes and suggestions that I have are, I think, good changes. I believe the things mentioned in this essay are the most important alterations for us to make and develop as a school. Recognizing the opinions of students, hiring quality teachers, and making our school safe are all vital parts of fixing our D.C. public schools.

***Alex Neeley*** *was born in 1994. Born and raised in Washington, D.C., he is the son of a Chinese American mother and an Irish American father. He currently lives with his mother, father, and older sister. He has great passion for writing, as well as a variety of sports. Alex enjoys spending time with his friends and family and volunteering in his community. After graduating high school, he plans to attend college, and dreams of using his love of sports and writing to become a sports journalist.*

# The New School

Katherine Rosenman, age 15
Washington, D.C.

As a student who is a visual learner, I would like to open my own school. It will be a place for those who have trouble just writing papers and reading from the book. The new school will help students learn in a different way, a way that lets them remember what they're learning. I will invent a school that specializes in the arts, meaning that it will have many good classes that teach all types of art, teach them in an "artsy" way, and have a very open and free aura. The point of the school will be to help those students who are having trouble learning the way most students do. The art will help bring a better understanding to the students so that they will be able to learn more about all the subjects.

There will be classes in everything from art history to geometry to jazz, open to students from grades nine through twelve. The school will focus primarily on visual learners, though other students may attend the school. As a faculty member, possibly even the principal, I will be sure that the students are learning because they will be taking fewer but more rigorous classes. Though they will have fewer subjects to study, they will do more work in those classes. The classes will change after the first semester. They will be normal subjects—just taught completely differently so that they form around the student's mind.

The classes will be taught in a creative way, meaning the students will be involved in projects that explain what they're learning. They will draw cells in biology and do art projects about M.C. Escher in geometry. Each class will be a scheduled class like history or math, but the way they are taught will bring out the more artistic side of the students. As visual learners, art will help them comprehend more about the subject. This approach includes all types of arts, anything from music to painting. Students will take eight classes a year: four the first semester, and then another four the second semester.

The building itself will be wide open and clean so that students will want to respect the facilities and will have plenty of space to concentrate. Preferably, the building will be modern, but if not, it will still be very open. Because students will be constantly assigned projects in their four classes, they will need plenty of room to spread out so that they can be inspired and determined to complete their work. Clearly, this will not be your average school, and it will require a reasonable amount of money to pay for all of the necessary supplies and to make the building. But the space will be ideal not only for the students but also for the teachers.

The new school will be a clean and liberating place in which students will excel in what they are good at. As a specialized school it will focus on the arts, and it will help them decide if they would like to pursue art or if they would like to pursue a career in math or in science. It will be the perfect place for a young mind to choose a pathway.

***Katherine Rosenman** is a high school sophomore in Washington, D.C. Though she was born in Chevy Chase, Maryland, she spent the first ten years of her life in Hillsborough, California, before moving back to D.C. Katherine enjoys drawing and various other arts. She wants to go to college to build on her art skills and hopefully, someday, become famous in the art industry.*

# Only DCPS

Kirby Sikes, age 15
Washington, D.C.

"Only DCPS." This is a phrase I hear at least once a week, referring to a disruptive, growling radiator or a defunct drinking fountain. It seems like everything at Wilson Senior High is broken. Students often complain about how dysfunctional our school is and how few resources we have. Having moved to Washington, D.C., from California, I know what a truly underfunded school is. The thing is, Wilson has lots of money and resources. District of Columbia Public Schools (DCPS) is one of the more highly funded school districts in the country. So where is all the money going?

A lot of money is spent on needlessly high energy bills. Our school building is kept at a steady 80 degrees Fahrenheit during the winter. I find myself sinking down under the blanket of heat and dozing off during my classes. Teachers realize that the heat is conflicting with our ability to think. Because of this, most classrooms have both the air-conditioning and the heater on at the same time. In addition to the air conditioners being loud and obnoxious, they are a waste of expensive energy. It already takes a lot of electricity to heat a large building, and when the air-conditioning and heater compete for dominance, it creates a black hole that sucks Wilson's money into utility expenses.

If I ran the school, I would turn the thermostat down to a practical and comfortable temperature and get rid of the security. Wilson also wastes its money on an ineffective security system. Every morning before entering the school, we have to go through metal detectors and send our backpacks through X-ray machines, which makes it difficult to get to class on time. Some days, almost half of my first period is late because security was slow. The security makes Wilson feel like a prison. Students don't feel trusted. I support school safety, but if somebody brought a gun or a knife into the school, the existing security wouldn't help very much. I have often hurried home after school to get sports things that I've forgotten for after-school practice. Every time I get back to school, less than forty-five minutes after school has ended, security has shut down, and I walk into the school without going through the metal detectors. Anyone who really wants to bring a weapon to school could come back after school and store it in their locker for the next day. If Wilson really needed security, then I would support having security that works. However, if Wilson needed security, then we would already see the dangerous consequences of our failing system.

With the money I'm not spending on heating and security, I would fix the broken drinking fountains and radiators as well as make other improvements. We also could take advantage of Wilson's location in the capital of the United States. Schools from all over the country take field trips to Washington, D.C., and get more out of the city's resources in a week than we get in a year. I would fund field trips to the Smithsonian institutions, the Capitol, the White House, and the embassies. Rather than sitting in class memorizing Islam's five pillars of faith, we could go on a field trip to a mosque or to the Saudi Arabian embassy. Rather than looking at our textbooks' photos of dinosaur fossils, we could see the real things at the Museum of Natural History. Congresswoman Eleanor Holmes Norton funds a program for high school students to visit Capitol Hill and watch congressional hearings and debates live. These experiences are things that my friends in California would kill for, but that we here in D.C. are missing out on.

Wilson could use the money to improve our library. At the

moment, the Wilson library is a cavernous room holding about ten bookshelves, all of them nearly filled with out-of-date books. A few wobbly study tables and fifty ancient computers with outdated word processors fill out the rest of the library. Wilson could buy some books to add to its meager shelves. We could buy new computers or at least install Microsoft Word on our current computers. The tables could be fixed so that students who come into the library can focus on studying instead of holding the table still while they write.

Wilson could expand its music program to offer not only jazz and choir but also a concert band and an orchestra. (I play cello and would love to participate in music at Wilson.) The chemistry classes could have the lab equipment needed to perform basic experiments. We could buy enough desks so that every student can sit during class. We could buy more health textbooks so that students aren't breathing on each other as they crowd around to read about disease control during class.

Most of Wilson's problems as a school come from money mismanagement. If Wilson would spend money on things that would really help the students, it would be a much better school. D.C. public schools are far from underfunded, and it is time for them to stop looking like they are.

***Kirby Sikes** is a high school sophomore in Washington, D.C. She was born in Washington but has lived most of her life in Berkeley, California, where her mother works as a law professor. She enjoys mountain biking and playing water polo. She hopes to go to UC Santa Cruz, where she will double major in math and philosophy.*

# Teacher, You Don't Understand Me!

Amyiah Alexander, age 19
Ann Arbor

You don't understand me. There are things that go on in my life that you don't know about. All you know is what goes on in your class. You don't know what goes on at home or in the halls. I feel like all you care about is what you want, like all your work being turned in on time and completed. I wish you would acknowledge that students have lives outside of school.

At school I am able to work hard in class, but that does not mean I am able to make the same full commitment at home. After school I am an athlete, a daughter, a crew member at McDonald's, a babysitter, *and* a student. Everything has its own level of responsibilities. Yet I have seven classes a day that all require homework.

First off, being a cheerleader is hard and exhausting. No matter what kind of day you have had, you have to push yourself to be the best in whatever athletic activity you are doing. Practices usually last about two-and-a-half hours, which does not leave me much time at home. If there is a game or tournament, it can last much longer, leaving even less home time.

At home I'm also a daughter—although that is not supposed to matter, because school is supposed to come first. I sometimes feel like my mother couldn't care less about that. I have to do the dishes for a house of seven, keep the two dens straightened, clean a bathroom, and pick up my room before I can go anywhere. If the chores don't get done, I get into a lot of trouble. Sometimes they take me all night, considering I have seven people living in my house and they all make messes.

Being a daughter is not just cleaning and chores, especially when you have younger siblings. I have two younger sisters and a younger brother. Being older, I am kind of the designated babysitter at home. My mom feels, "Why hire a babysitter when I have Amyiah?" I have to cancel my plans for my family, which isn't fair, because I'm not their mother.

About four days a week, I go to work at McDonald's after cheerleading practice. I work about four hours a day, which means I get off around 10 PM every night. Everybody thinks that working at McDonald's is simple—quite the contrary. They work you extremely hard for that minimum wage. Working there involves cleaning bathrooms, mopping floors, washing dishes (the greasy grill dishes are the worst), cooking, making sandwiches, and dealing with customers who are not always the nicest.

When I get home from work, I can't go straight to sleep, although I wish I could. The last part of my day is being a student. It involves long nights of studying for difficult tests. I cannot get around this without falling behind in classes. I stay up almost all night working on schoolwork, and then wake up at five in the morning. A lot of people say, "It's crazy that you wake up that early!" Well, if you live in a house with seven people, you want to be first in the bathroom, before there is no hot water. I can't continuously press snooze on my alarm clock, because if I do, there might be somebody in the bathroom by the time I finally get up. If that happens, I get behind on my schedule and have to pray that the other person is not using a lot of hot water.

If only we had more hours in the day. That would help. But we don't. So maybe if I talk to you, we could set up something. That works with some teachers. Others feel like they give enough time to do the work as it is, and there should be no excuses. Well, how do you determine that? Maybe if you give more time to do the homework, we could get it done. Giving us less work or not giving homework every day, or making homework due at the end of the week, also might help. Maybe we can even compromise on the amount of work, or the time available to get the work done. Please be more understanding of students, and help us help ourselves.

***Amyiah Alexander*** *is a senior from Ann Arbor, Michigan. She works at a McDonald's not far from her school. She is one of eight children in her immediate family. After high school, she plans to attend school in Louisiana because she feels that after Hurricane Katrina, it is the place that needs help the most. She plans to study forensic psychology to work with juveniles. She enjoys dancing, singing, cheering, and just hanging with friends.*

# Teachers, Our Last Salvation

Marie Angeles, age 18
Seattle

For the past seventeen years of my life I have moved from public school to public school, finding teachers who continually commit a crime against students. Teachers, specifically those who are middle-class and well educated and who enter public schools with low-income minority students, commit this crime without even being conscious of it. This crime is the idea that, as a middle-class and well-educated teacher, you have come to somehow "save" the students. However, this idea is wrong. You are not our last salvation.

Several times now, I have come across teachers who commit this crime of hubris without considering the consequences of their actions. To act as if you are teaching students who are in desperate need of salvation gives the impression that you don't believe in the students' ability to think and rescue themselves. You walk in and act as if you have come to save the "at-risk" youth in public schools from the common problems of their world. What do you get in return? We, the "at-risk" youth you've come to save, react negatively to, retaliate, and refuse everything you do and offer. We notice your condescending behavior and lose all respect for the teacher who shows it. I heard a teacher once say, "The school used to be better when there was busing, because now we just have students who don't know any better." To make matters worse, the comments never stopped; they became part of the teaching. Students were told that, compared to the teacher's parents, ours don't care as much, because that's just how things are now. The students were expected to sit there and absorb all of this as if it were a life lesson. The common response I've found to this behavior is "You don't know me" or "You don't know my life" or "You are not my parent," and we walk away and shout as we're saying it.

The question that comes to mind is: am I truly at risk of getting lost in the system without your help? The answer should be *yes*, but not in the way you think. Today the American dream has been reduced and replaced by the dream of just getting by. The least amount of work is now the only requirement to be successful. This dream has been subsidized by teachers who come in with low expectations of students' abilities and intelligence, and by public school districts that force thirty-two students onto one teacher and fail to provide sufficient resources for them. As a result of these other forces, the students themselves also live out this dream of just getting by.

You as a teacher, not as a savior, can prevent this. If you believe that you are a rescuer of sorts, you fail to fully comprehend what lies at the heart of the problem with students. If you don't understand a student's story or even that a story exists, you will continue to commit this crime against students. While learning about your students may not be 100 percent relevant to the subject you teach, it is 100 percent relevant to your success as a teacher as well as to the success of your students. When you don't understand why the students are the way they are, you start to belittle and berate them for their inabilities. You don't understand why they don't understand because you've simplified everything for "at-risk" minds, and you don't know what else to do but to berate and belittle. It seems to me you have forgotten your role as teacher.

Teachers, you are not our salvation; you are our facilitators. Your role is to equip us with the strategies to improve, not to remind us of our inabilities. Guide your students toward new discoveries and provide them with a way to understand the knowledge you are teaching, not just remember it for an exam. Give your students a desire to learn and do more than the minimum required. Do not enter a room full of students with doubt—instead, walk in with hope. If you truly wish to end this crime against students, you will come in not as our saviors but as the facilitators we need to truly learn the subject at hand—and more.

***Marie Angeles** is a senior in high school and was born in the Philippines. At the age of two, Marie moved to Hawaii with her adopted family. At the age of ten, she moved to Seattle, Washington, where she currently lives with her adopted mother. Marie has participated in theater and mock trials since the tenth grade. She enjoys writing and acting and plans to pursue both when she attends Scripps College in the fall. Her dream is to attend law school.*

# Raising the Standards

## Natalia Varela, age 18

Seattle

From experience, I know that encouragement from another person, especially a teacher, can help you achieve any goal. In my case, that meant enrolling in Advanced Placement (AP) classes. AP classes give students a key advantage, as colleges look favorably on these classes in applications. They demonstrate the student's dedication and passion for going beyond regular high school classes that require less work.

Unfortunately, although those classes open many opportunities for a student's future, they are not always accessible to everyone. Even though there was no minimum GPA requirement to enroll, I felt less prepared and less encouraged to take advanced classes than my peers were—until I moved to Bellevue.

The AP classes in my high school contain many more Caucasian students than Latino and African American students. You always have to consider that fewer minorities actually attend my school, but even then the enrollment numbers are not proportional to the demographics. Still, one AP teacher reached out and introduced AP classes to me and to many other minorities in my school. When I started my first AP class, I was intimidated, as I was the only Latina.

At the beginning of my freshman year, I attended a school in New Jersey that was considered a "school for slackers" by the rest of the county. I was obligated to attend since I lived within the school's district boundaries, but ever since my first days there I did not feel encouraged to do well. As a Latina, I was part of the majority at this school, and my fellow classmates and I showed no concern for our education by skipping every single week and sleeping in class. My teachers simply turned their backs on our flippant attitudes and continued with their lesson plans.

After six months in that school, I moved to Bellevue, Washington, where I immediately noticed differences in the educational system. Most of the students in my math class were taking notes, paying attention, and asking questions. My new teachers had very high expectations of me, and they encouraged me daily to achieve higher.

I met a teacher who deeply believes in empowering students because she said no one's potential should be lost in the cracks. It was because of her that I learned what an AP class was, and she encouraged me to take three. She understood that a student's motivation is not always fixed. I went from being a slacker to an A+ student after a lot of encouragement and goal-oriented thinking. Even if you have had a poor education, that does not determine how successful you might be in advanced classes. I recommend that teachers raise their expectations for all students so that precious potential will not be lost.

***Natalia Varela** was born in Bogotá, Colombia, in 1991. At the age of six, she moved from Colombia to New Jersey, where she lived for nine years. She enjoys dancing and spending time with her family. Her biggest goal is to become a doctor.*

# Making Mistakes and Learning

## Brian Curcio, age 15
Chicago

Life is about second chances, about making mistakes and learning. In first grade, if we got a problem wrong, the teacher would correct it. A fight on the playground would result in a time-out. People didn't look at us on a piece of paper but instead saw who we really were. Not anymore. Now, in high school, it feels to me as though teachers only care about the letters next to your name and your transcript. Once those are tainted, it seems as if you're dead to them. Why can't the world look past the sheets of black and white? Past the small characters that decide it all?

All my life, my parents have told me that I'm special, that my mind holds all of the world's possibilities. They have told me that I should be smart beyond books; that being people-smart is just as vital. People should be able to communicate with one another, not just test well. What's the point of good ideas if you can't express them well? I'd like to see a test for people-smarts.

In my freshman year, I was an academic mess. I had recently transferred, and for me meeting new kids in high school held a much higher value than my schoolwork. The border between work and play was so corroded that by the time my grades came around, they weren't promising. I knew I had more potential. My parents knew I had more potential. But all of the "possibilities" my parents said I had were vanishing before my eyes. The issue was that I was undermotivated and throwing my life away. But was that really the case? When I looked around at kids who were getting A's—the kids who stayed behind after class, the kids who raised their hands to speak—they never seemed happy. I wanted to be engaged, because at one point I do remember enjoying school, but between the worksheets and the monotonous lectures, the excitement of education was lost. I no longer caught the knowledge thrown at me and trapped it in my mind. Instead, I felt stifled by the information until I slipped into a daydream or the dismissal bell rang.

People aren't just computers that hear, memorize, and recite. Beneath the reiteration of facts, there are emotions. There is a person. Important studies in childhood education say that an engaged student will learn more, and I wonder: shouldn't the same hold true for a student who is happy? I believe that enjoying school is one of the benefits a student should receive from his or her education. If students are genuinely happy, they can learn more. My teachers have always tried to hammer information into my mind, but it only falls back out again after the test is taken. What would happen, though, if the teacher didn't have to simply cram in these facts, and kids were happy while learning? Excited by what they learned?

Everyone likes new knowledge. People like being smart. If schools could take a moment of self-reflection and think about how to truly engage a class, make the students *enjoy* that writing assignment, I'm sure that grades would improve. Beyond that, these graduates wouldn't just have memorized pages. They themselves would be books of knowledge—books with covers, titles, and emotions throughout. These students would transform from just chasing a grade to becoming a well-rounded person.

So many statistics put the blame on the students. Graduation rates, literacy rates—they all come back to the student. In reality, I believe that the root of this problem is that students are not being engaged by their teachers in class. Schools need to account for the students as people, not only as numbered takers of a standardized test. Teachers should use a range of styles in the classroom, incorporating technology and other tools to interest their students. Teachers should diversify their lesson plans not just from year to year but from class to class. For example, if a class has a specific interest in one of the topics, such as the Incas over the Mayans, then let that class study the Incas. It's my belief that every kid has the potential to learn. I've had friends who are failing and friends who are acing tests, and the only difference that I've observed is that the successful ones are engaged in school. Everyone has that switch. It's the teacher's job to find it and turn it on.

Unfortunately, most teachers face a major obstacle when it comes to teaching. They have national tests. From the way they have been described to me, these tests, which say who will succeed and who will fail, can take the once-bright spirits of a teen and crush them. These tests conform the very essence of who students are—of who I am—into the rigidity of categories and hierarchies.

In the strictly academic world they want me to live in, you don't get points for asking questions. One day in my history class, we were reviewing the rise of the Nazis. A friend of mine asked the teacher a question, wondering if the rise of the Nazi party was similar to the rise of certain groups in the Middle East. The relation from the past to the present seemed to bring the history to life. But the answer was "It doesn't matter; that's not on your test." So now when my friend goes home and his mom asks what he learned today, he can simply regurgitate the facts. How can a teacher turn away the curiosity of a student? For a student to raise his hand and try to relate—isn't that a teacher's dream? I've always thought the reason to study history was to learn from the past. How can we learn from the past if the present isn't "on our test"?

Rules are rules, and they cannot be broken. Teachers tell us that. Parents tell us that. Maybe it's because if people actually began to think about how our current system worked, then there would have to be change. God forbid anything changes; at the current graduation rate, everything must be perfectly fine. This isn't to say we need to do away with all rules and throw the education system into anarchy, but when you reflect on some rules, and the severity of what happens when they are broken, the figures on both sides don't seem to add up.

Throughout my entire education, I've pushed boundaries due to my intellectual curiosity. As long as I can remember, I've been praised at teacher conferences for my lust for knowledge. In sixth grade, I wanted to shape the fins on my bottle rocket differently, to see how the bottle would fly. It failed—miserably. But, for me, that wasn't the point. The crash landing isn't the part I remember. My memory is that I could build my rocket how I wanted, and that I could test whether it flew. At the age of eleven, I had the control to follow my curiosity and explore my own ideas, the ones that engaged me in my design technology class. As a result, I continued to love that class throughout school.

In this world, I've found that some people say one thing and mean another, while others don't mean anything. When it comes to the proverb "Kids will be kids," I don't think anyone actually thinks about what this implies. "Kids will be kids" refers to the fact that we all push boundaries and make mistakes. If adults—the rule makers of our system—always say this, then why isn't disciplinary action based on the same principle?

Throughout my education I've been friends with all types of kids: whiz-kids, student athletes, and troublemakers, to name a few. Of these kids, occasionally I lost a friend due to harsh, unrestricted disciplinary action against experimenting. The curiosity that we're told to have obviously will lead to kids occasionally trying out drinking, testing out new drugs. These are the little mistakes of adolescence. These miniscule mistakes held drastic consequences—consequences that most likely altered the course of their lives. The consequences altered their life in high school! Perhaps they were not kids? Or do certain missteps close off the opportunity for a second chance? Maybe the proverb "Kids will be kids," should have a little asterisk at the end, signifying that this applies only when the student's parents have enough money to cover the issue or when certain circumstances validate a second chance. In such a rigid system, broken rules shouldn't have multiple resolutions.

I don't know the answers to the rhetorical questions above. I can only slightly grasp the problems. I just don't understand how the basic morals we are taught as kids—that everyone is a unique person—doesn't hold true in a multiple-choice test. There is no bubble to fill in for "I enjoy my life and wake up with a smile." No box to tick for the number of close friends you have. Instead, we fill in bubbles for how much of our life we've signed away to work. Some kids go into that test and might have half their bubbles already gone if they broke a rule a year back, and opportunities that they deserve are cut off from them. They were curious. They thought outside the box. Unfortunately, the scanner can't read that. In fact, unless what you say is marked with a No. 2 pencil inside the inked lines, it can't read much of anything.

***Brian Curcio** is a rising high school junior. Although he was born in London, England, Brian has lived in Chicago since he was five years old. Football, basketball, and baseball are Brian's outward interests (depending on the season), while cooking and writing are his internal releases. Writing has always been a way to fuel his imagination, and recently Brian has made it a point to write with more purpose, expressing a desire to be heard outside his family walls. Poetry, music lyrics, and essay writing are his tools. Brian learned about 826 Chicago in 2009 and soon joined the Youth Advisory Board to help develop his writing skills.*

# Does It Matter?

## Brenda Carrillo, age 18

Seattle

When you have a connection with a student, you form a bond with them that will allow you to communicate more effectively with each other. On the other hand, if you have a poor relationship with a student, he or she is not going to look forward to your class or subject. In my experience, when I didn't get along with one of my teachers or felt they didn't care to talk to me, I was not interested in what they had to say or in trying to learn from them.

One of the best teachers I have had was open to what we had to say and was fun to be around. He joked with us, so everyone felt comfortable speaking up. He seemed to care about our outlook on many different subjects aside from AP English. Even a simple "How's it going?" or "What's wrong?" could really make a difference during the day. At first it felt weird to be asked about myself. I wondered: why does he care? He would call students at home to ask, "Why weren't you at school today?" We realized he was not a blank-faced teacher who lectured at us, who did not know us. He knew us well enough to realize that we would learn better if he got us interested in the subject. He truly seemed to care. I think this gave him a huge advantage in teaching: the more students are open to a teacher, the more that teacher can help you learn.

Keep in mind that when I say "open up to your students," I don't mean that a teacher should be a pushover: students can and do take advantage of teachers who are too open and forgiving toward their students. After that, it's hard for teachers to take back their authority. My AP English teacher could be tough, but he was fair and caring too, so when he got tough with us, we knew he did it because he wanted to help us.

It was different in my Spanish class junior and senior years. As a native Spanish speaker, I thought this would be an easy A. Though I knew I needed some help with refining my Spanish, I believed I had the basics down, and I would learn the rest by taking the class. When the class began, I asked many questions, because there were differences between what my parents were teaching me and what I was learning in class. For instance, my teacher would say certain phrases completely differently than how I had heard them at home. I was confused, but when I asked her why she said things in a certain way, she would answer tersely, "Because it's how you say it," and that was it. It felt as if my mom were saying, "Because I said so!" at home. Never being one to accept that explanation, I was irritated by my teacher's responses to my honest questions. It's as if she thought I was trying to outsmart her, when all I wanted was for her to guide me and clarify things for me. Instead, she would accuse me of arguing with her and order me to look the information up instead of answering my question. I realize that we both were very hardheaded, which made it very difficult for us to form a good relationship; all we did was disagree. But sometimes I felt as if she didn't even try to meet me halfway. I had hoped I would love this class because it would help me learn more about my native language, but because I had such a negative relationship with my teacher, I ended up detesting it. It was clear that we did not like being in each other's presence, and the relationship took a huge toll on my motivation to do well in her class, which affected my grade.

Teachers, ask yourselves: as a student, how would it feel to go through the motions of your school life, if you hate being there because of the relationships you have with your teachers? I know I hate going through school like that, feeling like no one cares. I realize that it is not going to be easy to form a connection right away with some of your students, and that sometimes it just won't happen at all. But I ask you to try, and try again, to reach your students to let them know you care not just about the subject you teach but about *them*. I know that if more of my teachers tried to make a human connection with me, I would find it a real advantage in learning. When I feel troubled and do not know what to do, it would be nice to be able to turn to a teacher for help. I believe that a teacher's responsibility is to let students know that they are willing to help, rather than leaving students afraid to ask.

When my teachers and I are not getting along, I sometimes don't even go to class. I bet that most students, including me, who skip class do so because we feel that all we do in class is argue with the teacher, who might even prefer that we weren't there. We would show up if we felt like you had time for us. But instead of listening to our queries for help, you repeat an empty "Come by after school, when I have time to deal with this." We students feel like you have given up on us, that you don't care about our education. You give off the vibe that we are wasting your time. I want you to know that such an attitude toward us doesn't just set us up for failure; you also set yourself up for failure as a teacher when you give up on us.

This is not to say that you are the only ones who need to change their attitudes. I realize that we as students have to meet you halfway. When I started to see that my grades in Spanish had dropped because I was spending more time arguing with the teacher than learning, I immediately talked to her and let her know that I cared about Spanish, and that I would be willing to do extra work so I wouldn't fail her class. I could tell right away that she sensed a change of attitude from me and softened up toward me a bit. She realized that I did care about her class, even though I had tried to tell her so all along. I tried to overcome my mistrust of her and open up; recognizing it, she opened up to me in turn. We did meet each other halfway after all.

That experience made me realize that when I build a wall between myself and my teachers, and I am blocking all the opportunities I have to learn. While a teacher cannot force a student to open up to them, they should definitely try. When students and teachers can be open and honest with each other, they have more respect for one another not only as teachers and students, but also as friends who have a goal in common, our learning. We understand how important having a good relationship with a teacher is and how it can help you in many ways, such as providing us with academic and job references, helping us find volunteer opportunities, and much more. But sometimes, we students are not certain whether we can trust you. We need you to make the first move. Show us you care, and we'll be sure to let you know we appreciate it.

***Brenda Carrillo** was born in 1992. She lives in White Center, Washington, with her parents, who are Mexican. Brenda enjoys learning new things and challenging herself to exceed her goals, and hopes one day to travel the world to make new materials, learn different cultures, and see many different aspects of life. She plans to take time off before going to college, but she is sure that she will do something in criminal justice. She is extremely motivated to become a police officer in Seattle one day.*

# 5

# "Tomorrow's Leaders" Speeches in the Voices of Secretary of Education Arne Duncan, President Barack Obama, or the Students Themselves

In many ways, every student in this book is giving a speech to an enormous audience. In this chapter, students took on the voice of our president, our secretary of education, or themselves, and articulated their insights into schools, teaching, learning, and leadership. Given that they are tomorrow's leaders, we're pleased with the results, and we think you will be, too. We look forward to reading your speech.

# For All

Marlin Quintanilla, age 17
San Francisco

Starting before integration
Before education was meant for all
The time of *Brown v. Board*
Until today
I haven't seen much change

Yes, they let us browns into schools
But the quality of education isn't the same

Our books are still ripped
And the pages are still missing
The teachers lack in their passion
And the kids are still ditching

They try to place the blame on lack of resources
But why us?
Why do we have to lack in the materials
That are supposed to be for all?

It's the education system
The unspoken Jim Crow laws

It's because God left us in the oven
For a little too long

History traces back the roots
Where our schooling was done in the streets
Where the great empires were
The Aztecs
The Mayas
And the Incas
Where math was done by counting
How many days we didn't eat
Or how many of our warriors had been killed

English was seen in the secret notes
We would leave behind
That only our families could read
Or in the writing on our bodies
That showed where we lived
And science was composed of strategic plans
Of Underground Railroads
In which we could escape and find a new life
School
The stepping stone to the ladder of success
Has only been acquired by a few
Because the places I've seen
With broken-down desks and unwanted youth
Are the stepping stone
For the next institution us browns are destined to go to

They'd rather spend the money sending
African and Latino American males
To a place they call jail
Where society has driven us to go
But we already know

I realize that this is not the path for me
My Richmond streets may cradle me in her arms
But they will not trap me
I will not choose the dead-end streets
But make right turns
My destination is across the Richmond Bridge
To a school behind a gate
In a community where browns can be counted
On my own two hands
My school has books that hold full pages
Teachers that are meant to do just that
Teach

But what they don't know is that
I teach them
That I bring two cultures to the classroom
Latina American
The true history of my people
The mathematical understanding of real life
My English that dances with my Spanish accent
And the scientific understanding
That I should not be standing before them

I live out what *Brown v. Board* was supposed to do
I go against Jim Crow and his laws
I go against all boundaries
I open doors
And live out my parents' dream

I am what education is supposed to be

***Marlin Quintanilla*** *is a high school senior from Richmond, California. In the fall of 2010, Marlin started her freshman year at*

*UC Riverside. Marlin plans to major in psychology and minor in creative writing. Her dream is to become a neuropsychologist or behavioral psychologist. She is inspired by her family members, who have taught her always to chase the impossible. Marlin enjoys sports, being outdoors, writing, baking, and just having a good time.*

# Our Children, Our Role

Madeleine Buck, age 17
San Francisco

It is the fundamental responsibility of our leaders and others in positions of power to ensure that every generation is well prepared for its role as citizens to participate in the decision-making process. A well-rounded education is the key element to achieving that goal. Each child has the right to be given the fundamental tools to make informed decisions and be taught the critical-thinking skills necessary to be a fully active member of his or her community.

Our teachers' jobs have been made more difficult and more challenging because they have had to assume a role in children's lives previously held by parents and other community members. This enormous task has been further compounded by increasingly drastic cuts to education funding, and, in turn, by the mixed messages sent to students—not only on fiscal but also psychological issues. This country's neglect of its young people is producing a generation that equates learning with the ability to fill in the correct bubbles and assumes that their growth as students, as citizens of the world, is inconsequential. By diverting funds away from education, lawmakers reveal the priorities of the shortsighted society into which students must learn to integrate themselves.

We must now move beyond using test scores as a measure of student achievement. In our desire to focus on the fundamentals, we have too often neglected other elements essential to a well-rounded education. The arts, the sciences, and after-school programs—areas that are always the first to be cut in a budget crisis—are frequently regarded as "dispensable," even though research and past practice have shown these programs to be equally critical to student success as the three R's. While test-taking is an inescapable part of school, test performance is not the only indicator of aptitude in a person, nor a valid measurement of someone's value as a human being.

Learning extends beyond its "textbook" definition, and the acquisition of knowledge should be a pleasure in itself. The success of such programs as Alice Waters's Edible Schoolyard in Berkeley, California, and the teacherless New Country School in Henderson, Minnesota, indicates the variety of educational opportunities presented by the use of less traditional educational models.

The United States currently spends more money on its prisoners than on its students. According to the U.S. Department of Justice, a staggering 75 percent of federal inmates did not complete high school. Just as federal budgeting reflects an inability to get to the root of the issue, the blame does not entirely lie with the high schools. A strong elementary education is crucial to dropout prevention, and the foundation established in these formative academic years rests in the ability to read. More than 20 percent of adults read at or below a fifth-grade level—far below the level needed to earn a living wage. I intend to establish a nationwide literacy program that ensures that all children, by the time they reach the third grade, will be able to read at grade level. As is, 21 million Americans can't read at all, 45 million are marginally illiterate, and one-fifth of high-school graduates can't read their diplomas.

I urge the federal government to subsidize all literacy programs, as well as do research to determine which prove the most effective. Bilingual education should be emphasized; studies show that children who learn to read in their native language have more success learning a second one, and, in an era of globalization, it is essential to be not only a citizen of the United States but also a citizen of the world.

We must not be afraid to take bold steps in our attempts to create a fully literate society. In making our country truly egalitarian, we must neither discount less traditional educational models nor maintain that current educational practices cannot be adapted to meet our goals. Our children are society's most valuable and vulnerable individuals; we must do everything in our power to provide for and protect them. It is tempting, in this country's current state, to concentrate only on the issues at hand that will directly affect our lives. While ending foreign involvement in the Middle East and finding solutions for domestic economic problems are both pressing issues, it is important to keep in mind the cyclical nature of our decisions: we still need to address the educational needs of today's students, because they are, above all, tomorrow's leaders.

***Madeleine Buck** is a high school junior. She is a visual art major and spends a lot of her time painting. She loves rock music.*

# The Concerns of Schools: A Speech in the Voice of Secretary Arne Duncan

Yuhana Gidey, age 17
Washington, D.C.

When addressing the concerns of schools, it is only right to mention the issues of all students within the school. I would first like to address all students and then focus on the disenfranchised students. Certain students, such as English Language Learner (ELL) students, get little recognition when it comes to making improvements for students. After visiting a D.C. public school, I saw much room for adjustment.

Allowing students to fail a course should be completely out of the question. Although it is the students' fault for lacking the initiative to do homework, read and conduct research, and go to class, it is the administration's fault for not reinforcing the importance and value of education. Many times when students fail, they lack the encouragement and resources they need to succeed. Students earning poor grades (C– and below) that reflect their struggles should have the additional one-on-one help they need. This is why, as the U.S. Secretary of Education, I plan to introduce a mandatory mentoring and tutoring program to the Board of Education as well as to the administrations of schools nationwide.

I have seen the improvement of urban areas resulting from neighborhood after-school programs. Students who attended these programs learned to strive for and achieve success. Through similar programs, I know there is reason to hope all students will be able to prosper and flourish, blooming into blossoms from buds. I was given the opportunity to have a tutor help me with certain subjects and courses, and I found this to be a great help. When my math skills and reading-comprehension skills strengthened, I felt reassured about the content and quality of my work and I knew that I was now in a position to help others in turn. To see other students progress with my help gave me a real sense of satisfaction; not only was I proud of myself for helping them, but I was also proud of the students who were able to understand the material and feel confident with themselves. I loved the connection and the comfort level the students had with me; those qualities allowed them to be open and willing to participate and engage with me. I feel the bond between students may be much stronger and more effective than that between an adult and student. Pairing a lowerclassman with an upperclassman and high school seniors with college students will help students get through school and the college application process. We would want many colleges participating in this mentoring program in order to give all students the opportunity to have mentors. Nobody would feel neglected.

Another issue of great concern is that students are often not aware of the requirements they need to fulfill to graduate from high school. At this stage in life, they need to be guided and provided with information. At my own school, the graduation requirements were not specified until senior year, when it was too late for many students to meet them. The factors and issues that will affect a student's ability to earn a high school diploma should be addressed in his or her freshman and sophomore years. Informing students only when it is too late to make a difference, or that they need to take a class that is no longer available, is not helpful whatsoever. While students may still be obliged to make up classes in the summer, because it might be too late to add or drop classes, we can do our best to help students avoid this situation. This should be the role of the counselors, as well as the administration, which leads me to the next topic.

Some students are disproportionately affected by current problems within school because they do not receive the attention they should. I have a solution for them. During my own time in high school, ELL students distanced themselves from other students, typically because they found it easier to communicate with one another. I have decided that there should be an adult who speaks their language to help them. These students tend to feel comfortable with each other because they come from similar backgrounds. They will be assigned a counselor or adviser to help guide them throughout their high school years. This counselor should have certain qualifications, including being bilingual or trilingual. ELL students would feel more of a connection and be willing to actually visit and talk to their counselor if they share a language and, if possible, a cultural background. They deserve to know someone who is capable of understanding them.

I hope the process of change will not take long. This vision will help every student, at every school, excel. Doing well, excelling, and being inclusive of all students are hard work, but never impossible. We, America, can make this happen.

***Yuhana Gidey*** *is Eritrean American, born and raised in Washington, D.C. She is a senior in high school and will be attending George Washington University in the fall. She plans to major in psychology. She has been an active martial artist, having taken tae kwon do for ten years, and has played soccer since elementary school. She has been involved in programs such as the Phase Campaign, Teen Women in Action, Peer Mediation, and student government (serving as treasurer). Two of Yuhana's most life-changing experiences are being a National Cathedral Scholar and being a member of the Peaceful Warriors, a martial arts demo team. She believes the keys to life success are family support, hard work, dedication, and persistence.*

# The Proper Tools to Prosper

Tinsley Harris, age 15
Washington, D.C.

The pressure on schools and students is rising. They are bombarded with the worries of class rankings, GPAs, standardized tests, and attendance rates. To overcome these pressures and achieve success, schools must start with simple tools. Success begins with the effort and time teachers and schools put into helping students expand their knowledge. What is effective for guiding students is lacking in schools: an abundant supply of updated textbooks and library books. High GPAs and standardized test scores and superlative attendance come with time. What today's students need is access to the right materials to prosper.

Without the proper tools, a classroom cannot function. If parents wouldn't send their children to school without paper and pens, why would school boards allow schools to operate without textbooks? Textbooks are essential to a teacher's curriculum. Without them, countless pieces of information are lost. At the same time, textbooks should not be a teacher's sole tool. Instead, used as an aid, textbooks provide key notes and help in objective comprehension, with section reviews, study guides, and practice tests. They also provide hands-on projects for students, which help reiterate the subject studied.

Providing learners with new textbooks has always been a struggle. Although school budgets are tight, it would be in the schools' best interest to supply adequate textbooks. Many of the textbooks in classrooms across the nation are hanging by a thread, literally. Hand-me-down books are not tools for success. At Woodrow Wilson High School in Washington, D.C., a health class suffered due to a lack of textbooks. Not only did a combined class of about sixty students have to share a set intended for twenty, the books were missing covers and numerous pages. Every day more books would disappear. Students were not able to complete their work sufficiently when they continually had to pass their books back and forth. All students need and deserve their own textbooks.

Library books are good aids for teachers as well. They include class sets of books regularly taught by teachers. Whether these books are needed for monthly book reports or related to the subject of interest, they are necessary. For example, an English class would not be complete without book reports. It would be much more convenient to have the books on hand for students rather than leave it to them to scramble to find them on their own. At the beginning of the year, teachers could request class sets of books they plan to have their students read. When used in conjunction with a lesson's themes, a class set of books will help students get a clearer understanding of what they are learning. While studying the Holocaust, for example, students could get a better understanding of its horrors by reading *Anne Frank: The Diary of a Young Girl*, along with historical fiction such as *The Devil's Arithmetic*, *The Boy in the Striped Pajamas*, or *Number the Stars*.

The school library should also carry regular books for students to check out. When a school library has an ample variety of books, it will draw lots of readers. If students know their library has hundreds of books, they will be more inclined to visit the library regularly. Students will feel their school took the time to consider their interests by carrying many genres of books. For students who do not own encyclopedias, they will find researching for projects an easier, stress-free task with a well-stocked library. Increasing the number of readily available books will also help raise test scores. Reading for pleasure, instead of constantly filing students into a room to bubble in circles, will lead to an improvement in not only the English portion of tests, but mathematics as well. Frequent reading will enhance students' vocabulary and reading rate, as well as help with analyzing word problems.

Any type of change, big or small, will be a challenge for schools. Knowing which goals to attack first, and how, is the most important step. Before we start the process, we must have our tools for improvement in place. If students are given the proper tools, success will follow. Textbooks provide vital information and check comprehension with learning exercises. Library books reinforce concepts taught in class and provide students with a form of entertainment that benefits them. Coupled together, this dynamic duo is the seed to success. Once students have mastered the information, they can use it to raise test scores, improve their grades, and obtain the greatest success possible: confidence in themselves that they are knowledgeable and can advance in any subject.

***Tinsley Harris** is a high school sophomore in Washington, D.C., where she was born and raised. She enjoys photography, reading, and writing poetry. She plans to attend college to study psychology and French. She also plans to publish her works in the near future.*

# How It Feels to Be on That List

Yolanda Jordan, age 13
Chicago

In the fifth grade, I moved from Memphis to Chicago to have a better education. Andersen was my first school in Chicago. It took me a while to adjust to being away from home, but eventually I grew to love it. Classes were led by very well-educated teachers. Partway through the year, however, we got the news that our Andersen was going to be phased out.

Our teacher was reading her email, and we were about to begin our daily writing. She told us there were going to be some changes coming, and that they were thinking about phasing us out. She told us we should write about how we felt about this in our journals. It is a horrible feeling, not knowing if your school is closing or staying open. All of us were angry that our school might not be there the next year, and we knew we had to fight to keep it open.

Let me tell you about the whole process. First, the school board puts the news on your school's website so that everyone will know what is about to happen. Then, they tell the students to take a letter home to their parents so that they will know what to do. Next, the board sends a representative to your school, so they can talk to the staff and parents. In my experience, you feel like you are talking to a brick wall. The day that the representative came to our school, I attended both the parent meeting and the student meeting. The student meeting was held in the evening, so we could be in class during the day, and the parent meeting was held during the morning, so the adults could meet and discuss whatever they need to after their meetings.

The day of the meetings, I went with my grandmother to the parent meeting in the morning, because I was working on a speech for the Board of Education. During the student meeting that night, it was as if I had no say and all I was supposed to do was listen. A lot of students were screaming. "What about gym classes and other extracurricular activities?" one boy yelled. The woman in charge would only respond that our questions would be addressed at the end of the meeting. Her eyes were like rocks; there was nothing there but coldness. At the end, she never answered our questions. She just said, "The meeting's adjourned." When I left the meeting that day, I felt very angry because there was a woman and man basically telling us how they were going to get rid of us.

The school held a protest downtown, and we circulated a petition to try and get more people in the community involved with helping the school stay open. At the protest, we had a sign saying, "If you believe we should stay open, honk your horn." We had all types of people honk—some didn't, but that didn't stop us.

All of these events led up to the big meeting that would decide it all. I went to speak at the Board of Education meeting in defense of my school. At the beginning, they handed out rules and regulations and told us if we took too long or if people began getting too angry we would be removed. I think about a hundred people spoke that night. We were one of several schools on the list trying to stay open. Most of our school's students were at the meeting, and all of us wore red shirts that read "United We Stand."

When it was my turn to speak, I was a nervous wreck. I was the first kid to speak because a lot of kids who were called on got too scared to go before these hairy, scary people. A lot of kids ended up having their parents go up to speak instead, but when it came to me, I looked at my grandmother, and she asked, "Are you ready to go?" It took me a minute to prepare, but I knew I needed to do this. All the other kids were backing out, but I wanted to be different. I wanted to do this. I looked back at her and answered, "Yes. I'm ready."

My speech was about how Andersen had been around for nearly 113 years, adding teachers and teachers and teachers. And not only teachers—think of the students! There was a real history there. Years ago, my dad was in room 212 in Andersen, the fifth-grade classroom, and when I first came to Andersen, I was put in 212 with my teacher Mrs. Ziegler. Every day of that year, I kept thinking, "Oh, my God, right now I'm probably standing in the same spot my dad used to stand in!" History is made at school. I wanted to have that same history. My school is like a rock that has to keep on rolling—you would never be able to stop it.

In the end, they voted to phase out my school and replace it with another branch of a school called LaSalle. LaSalle is a magnet school that pulls in kids from around the city to work on reading, writing, and math. We were told that LaSalle was chosen because it had more students. A "small school" can hold up to 900 students, and a "large school" can have up to 2,000. We had about 350 students in our school at the time, and the school board said we weren't using enough of our space.

Here were tons of people cheering for our school, but the members of the school board still put that gavel down. I had so much rage against the board that day. It felt to me as though they had taken away all my history. They had basically said, "Andersen, you are *gone*, we're phasing you out, and you can't stay here." Taking away our entire school? You just can't do that. It's not right. The students who have been forced to leave their school really cared about it. If you take a good look at me or any of the kids from Andersen, all you are going to see is pain. You have kids who had been going there since kindergarten. Or the newer kids who feel that they have been tossed from school to school, and now think, "You're still going to toss me around?"

By moving students around in this way, you are forcing kids into bad neighborhoods and gigantic schools. Some people think that closing a school is right, but look at it from a child's perspective. To be in a new school and have to make new friends is hard, and it's especially hard to have to start over. If you squeeze certain kids together, especially girls, they are not going to share lockers easily, and there are going to be major conflicts. There are going to be cliques. And what about all the staff members? In the long run, aren't you going to have to hire more? There will be more of everything, and it's going to mean a different, bigger job.

A class that is too big is a bad thing. If there are thirty-two kids in a class, you're not going to be able to get them to listen to you. You're not going to know all of their names. Students are not able to get one-on-one help from the teacher for their specific needs—needs that someone else may or may not have. Small schools allow for more personal connections. Students know almost every other student, and this builds a great community. Teachers know their students on a more personal level, too. Going to a smaller school lets teachers know how each student works. This makes learning much easier because teachers know how to work with students and who to pair us with, and they are available for extra help if needed.

You have to think of the parents, too. It is good for the teachers to know the parents as well; this improves parent participation and creates a stronger school community. They are the ones who have to drive their kids to school everyday. Do you think they like taking time out of their busy schedules to bring their kids to new, faraway schools? Most of the time, when the board closes a school, they don't send you to a nearby school; instead, they suggest you go to a school farther away. Yes, there are buses, but they don't come out very far, which leaves a lot of kids without a ride. And if students don't have a ride, well, I guess they can tell the state, "You said, 'No child left behind.' "

What is going to happen to that student? We are students, not numbers or visual aids or statistics. When I went to the meeting held by the Board of Education, they referred to us as "the little dots." They were drawing dots up on the board to represent us, and they were showing parents how they were going to break up these dots and send us to different schools. This became kind of a joke for me, and I started saying to everyone, "Hello, little dot! Hey, little dot!" The board representatives explained at the meeting how this group of little dots would go to *this* school and another would go to *that* school and so on. But each dot on that board was a kid who would have to give something up so that she or he could go to school.

Here's a bit about me: My name is Yolanda. I love to write. I do. I *love* to write. I'm a cheerleader for the Bulldogs, and I'm pretty good. (I have a nice pike jump.) I have three terrific brothers who get on my nerves all the time. I have a lot of friends. Corrie and Marla are my best friends, because they're silly and funny and weird, and I am, too. They fill my whole day with laughter and joy. I go to 826 Chicago for tutoring because I like to write, and I'm terrible at math. Some people think it's weird, but I love broccoli, no cheese, just cooked. To me, it tastes like nature. But I hate brussels sprouts. I just found out I snort sometimes, because I just snorted out loud as I was writing this. (I did. I've never done it before!) I love winter because my birthday is in the winter, when I turn a year older and get a year closer to eighteen, when I can vote and stop world hunger. My favorite song is "Candy Kisses" because I think it's sweet, but I can't remember who sings it. I look up to Tyra Banks because she gives so many people opportunities to do something great. And I really look up to my mom, who is strong and knows how to hold her tears through everything—and I mean everything. I want to be an OB-GYN or a midwife when I grow up because I love babies and I want to check up on the moms and be there with them, and I think that's cool.

I wonder, now. Do you really think, readers, that I'm just a dot?

At the end of fifth grade, my grandmother sent me to stay with my mother and to go back to school in Memphis, to see how it would work out. My grades weren't as good as they had been at Andersen, so I came back to Chicago in January, two days before my birthday.

At that point, it was so late in the year that my grandmother decided I would not go back to Andersen. Instead I went to Peabody, which was my neighborhood school.

Before I went to Peabody, I was really nervous about starting a new school, but then I met people I really liked. I liked the teachers because they were educated and they explained who they were and how they worked. I also liked the students. They were friendly and open and warm. I had a great year at first.

Close to the end of the year, though, we were on "the list" again. This time, though, they were not deciding whether or not to phase out the school. Instead, they were considering closing it outright. Everybody from other schools was asking us, "What are you going to do?"

To readers, I say this: Communities can get involved in helping schools stay open. Members of a community need to support community schools and make the connections needed to keep them open. People who live in the schools' neighborhoods can help out with programs after school. Instead of sitting at home, people could start athletic programs, newspapers, newsletters, and other activities that could help students. So much depends on getting the word out to the community about what is happening in the schools and letting them do what they can do to help out.

***Yolanda Jordan*** *is from Memphis, Tennessee. Her parents are Shawn and Nikita Bass, and she has three brothers and one sister—they are really cool people. They make Yolanda laugh a lot. Yolanda has a fish named Ben who she thinks is a boy (she's not sure, though). Yolanda loves to write. She thinks that 826 Chicago has given her a great chance to show her talent. She'd like to write a book by age thirty-five. Yolanda's favorite color is purple and she loves chocolate. She also loves to play with newborns; they're just so cute.*

# Obama's Speech

Kaitlyn Pieske, age 16
Ann Arbor

Good evening. I hope all of you are having a very nice day. I have been thinking about ways to change our children's education, and I have come up with some good solutions.

The first issue I want to address is the school environment. It's hard for many people to concentrate on schoolwork when they don't have a calm, clean, and organized environment to work in. A second issue is funding. We need more funding for our children's education, to buy things such as updated books and computers. Finally, attendance is a key issue we need to address to ensure a good education. We must do something to help our students to stay in school and show them how important it is for their future. I will provide a variety of resources for the students who aren't doing well in school, such as mandatory tutors and teachers able to stay late and help students. We must show them how much education is needed, and we must improve these issues to do it.

I believe all of our children in the nation should have a calm, clean, and well-organized environment to learn and work in. Our children need to feel comfortable in the place where they learn and work. Schools with an unhealthy environment will have more failing students. Children can be more focused on their schoolwork if they are in calm environments with less noise and commotion.

Every superintendent should develop a plan for their teachers' organization so it will not interrupt our children's education. Each superintendent should check on every school in the district at least every two months to ensure the organization plan is working well. They should also check the cleanliness of the school and hold a meeting with all students on the importance of keeping their school clean. Working in a dirty environment is distracting and often very unhealthy.

Most schools don't get enough funding for the essential things they need to teach. Many students are falling behind in their education due to the lack of funding, which prevents some students from getting a higher-level education and others from getting an education at all. It all depends on the location of the school and the funding it receives. This is not what education is about. Some schools don't even have enough money to purchase books for their students. Other schools have more funding and use it to the full extent by purchasing current books and laptops and remodeling parts of the school.

I, Barack Obama, have a plan for your children's future. I am going to improve their education by making sure every school gets the decent amount of funding needed to provide a proper education for every one of its students. Two weeks before the end of every school year, all teachers will write papers describing ways to improve their schools. I am promising to keep an eye on the education of our children, and I am determined to make education better. By the end of 2010, every school in the United States will have enough books. Schools that can't afford updated books will be given them. We, the people, must find a way to change this disparity, to change the way our students are learning, and to prevent them from losing out on their education.

Truancy has become a big issue, one that is affecting the education of our nation as a whole, and we need to put a stop to it immediately. Attendance is very important, especially when you're in high school. Our students sometimes choose to hurt their own education by skipping class, failing to complete homework and classwork, or being insubordinate with their teachers. This is hugely disappointing, because these things can be prevented and addressed so they do not become an ongoing problem. When students skip class, the first thing the staff usually does is contact the students' parents. I don't think this works for every student as well as it should. Some parents enforce discipline better than others. In most cases this works out, but in other cases not as well as it should.

When a student skips too much school, the school will try to expel the student or deny her credit for the classes she did pass. This is not the way things should be handled. I believe every student in every public school in the United States should have a discipline plan to address all of his or her insubordinate actions. We are trying to help the students who are struggling, not kick them out because the school is worried the student will hurt the school's reputation. Their reputation would improve if they kept those students in school and helped them turn around—by helping them improve their grades, encouraging them to attend class regularly, and showing them where they can turn if they need extra help with something.

There are plenty of ways that we can reach out to our students and help them achieve more in school. I suggest assigning a mandatory mentor for students who can't keep up with their schoolwork or are receiving failing grades. Schools should come together as a whole and work together for greater success—so, for example, a member of each department (such as math, English, science, and social studies) should be required to stay late after school. Then we can require failing students to stay after school to study or receive extra help or even just do their homework. When the mentor and the teacher see improvement in the student's grades or performance, they can have a meeting with the student and his or her parents to decide if he should continue the program or work independently again.

We, the people of the United States, will no longer let our children suffer from the lack of education. We see a much more promising future for the education of our children. Thank you all for your time, and have a very enjoyable day.

***Kaitlyn Pieske*** *is a high school junior in Ann Arbor, Michigan, where she was born and raised. She works at a Meijer store and attends school full time. Kaitlyn enjoys reading, writing, listening to music, and spending time with her family and friends. After high school, she plans to attend Ross Medical School so she can become a medical assistant. She plans to become a nurse specializing in the NICU (neonatal intensive-care unit) because she loves children so much. She dedicates her essay in this book to Kinah and Evee.*

# Afterword: "I Didn't Know You Talked Like That"

## Pirette McKamey*

I love all the languages English allows us to speak: those of intellect, of humor, of love. I am particularly intrigued by youth language—some of it. I love it when Dewayne Davis says, "You're puttin' too much on it"; when Brianna Frank calls something *jenky*; and when Angie Colon-Chin lets me know who's phony and who's not.

Youth language only concerns itself with youth issues. High school students care a lot about who is focusing attention on them, and so *puttin' too much on it* can be an admonition to a peer who won't let something go or praise for a teacher who won't let them go. *Jenky* has been around for a long time and means exactly what it sounds like. *Phony* is an interesting one because some students only know it in the context of their vernacular.

When I recently told one of my students, Cindy Tuala, that I hoped something wasn't phony, she said, "I didn't know you talked like that."

* *Pirette McKamey is an experienced, effective educator. And we believe she's a San Francisco hero. She brings magic to her classroom while keeping her expectations of her students tremendously high. In 2010 she was invited to speak at an 826 Valencia event about youth writing and her experience welcoming community volunteers into her classroom. Pirette's speech was so moving and so eloquent that we asked her if we could share it with you. We're thrilled to have an educator's perspective in our anthology, and we believe it will inspire you.*

"Like what?" I asked.

She said, "In slang. Like us."

"But *phony*'s a real word, Cindy," I said.

She said, "No, it's not. Really?"

The word *phony* has been claimed by our youth and so has its opposite, *real*. Young people are always trying to figure out what's real and what's not, who's authentic and who's not. It means a great deal to them.

What 826 Valencia offers to students is decidedly real, and by *real* I mean that the work gets done. With the help of 826 tutors, students write and think and puzzle over their own words, rewriting and getting so involved in the process that they forget that they thought they couldn't write in the first place.

For months they do it; they write. They create writerly experiences and develop a body of work that defines them as writers. So the evidence mounts, and most of the students are willing to face these truths: they are writers because they write, and to become a writer one must write.

Now the question is: what compels these students to stay engaged with their own thinking and writing over a multidraft process? Many say genuine purpose or an audience, such as writing for publication in a book. I know it is more complex than that. A student will take a twenty-minute journal entry written for points in a World Literature course as seriously as a five-page class anthology if her work is honored and her thoughts, musings, and ideas are heard.

Students who work with 826 Valencia tutors, editors, and directors feel honored and heard at every stage of the writing process, from brainstorm to polished product, precisely because their work is honored and their voices are heard—and that is by design.

For my class of juniors at Mission High School, the design looked like this: after a summer of thinking, planning, and organizing, twenty to forty 826 Valencia tutors came to my classroom almost every class period for over three months to work with students individually. They came on Monday, returned on Tuesday, and again on Thursday. They repeated this pattern over and over. The students came to depend on the tutors. The tutors—of diverse ages, ethnicities, interests, and understandings of what makes good writing—sat in the computer lab next to the students for one hundred minutes each class period, read over the students' work, listened to the students talk, and made suggestions for improvement. The tutors made errors in judgment, and the students forgave them. The students were absent, and the tutors forgave them. The students learned to trust the tutors. In this way, the students' potential was coaxed forward.

The people who plan and implement the youth programs at 826 Valencia know about writing—that it has the power to transform and soothe as well as entertain and inform—and about teaching and learning—that our intellect is as intimate to us as our emotion—and therefore they craft programs that actually change the students and the teacher. When students are supported and find success by publishing a written piece of work in a book, they have met their potential. For a moment in time, there is a resting place beyond the realm of possibility. They are in the realm of being. For a moment, they are simply being. And that feeling of being is one they will never forget and one they will seek to re-create, whether through writing, dancing, fathering, doctoring, or toiling beneath the hood of a car.

***Pirette McKamey** has taught middle school history and high school English and drama for over twenty years, and became the educational reform facilitator at Mission High two years ago. She spent four years instructing future teachers at the University of San Francisco and has served as a consultant for the Bay Area Writing Project since 1993. Pirette and her students at Thurgood Marshall High and Mission High have worked with 826 since it opened in 2002 on projects ranging from personal statement workshops to larger publishing projects such as the* Mission High Magazine.

# Some Suggestions for Making Classroom Publishing Projects Work

Publishing student work is one of the central activities of 826—honoring students' accomplishments, giving them an opportunity to develop and then show off their skills, and enhancing the quality of their writing. We create all kinds of publications, large and small, and in all genres: journalism, cartooning, poetry, historical fiction, and on and on. Some publications are written and printed in a single workshop; others take an entire semester. Each time we dive into a student-publishing project, however, we follow the same basic guidelines.

First, our projects always begin with the teachers. We ask teachers about their goals for their classrooms, and we then try to create projects that will fulfill them. While our projects are often ambitious and multifaceted, they are meant to complement or enhance the work the teachers are already doing with their students.

826 and our partnering teachers develop projects that give students the chance to collaborate both with adults and with peers. Students work with designers, editors, and writers who bring the literary and professional world into the classroom. At the same time, we encourage kids to read each others' work and give feedback and suggestions. Of course, the real magic of these collaborations rests in the guidance and undivided attention the tutors give their stu-

dents; we ask our volunteer tutors to share their love of writing and their belief that hard work can be joyful.

826 projects place students in decision-making roles. When students are at the helm, their investment deepens and the learning sticks. Rather than being assigned tasks that are later assembled into a finished project by adults only, the student-authors help steer the overall writing and editing process. They select book covers, organize chapters, and work with professional designers. They enjoy a robust apprenticeship experience that is satisfying and real.

By publishing and distributing the books, 826 is able to reach a broader audience of readers or listeners beyond the students' schools. We show the students that there are eyes and ears beyond their teachers, parents, and immediate peers; this bolsters their pride, showing that their work means something even outside the classroom walls. The book you are holding is evidence of 826's commitment to placing classroom projects within a final, finished, and professionally made product—a beautiful object that dignifies the students' work and makes the learning experience tangible.

826 projects challenge students to address real-life problems and questions. Like the writers in this book, other 826 students have grappled with serious themes, such as creating peace in a violent world, immigration and migration, and reflections surrounding family and home. We've seen that complex topics motivate the students to perform at a higher level and help them understand how writing can be meaningful and relevant to their own lives.

Feel free to reach out to the teams at 826 for further suggestions. Good luck with your publication! Send us some of your student essays, and we'll publish them in our student gallery on the website at www.826national.org.

# About the Editors

**Nínive Calegari** *is the co-founder of 826 Valencia and 826 National. She is a veteran public school teacher and a co-author (with Daniel Moulthrop and Dave Eggers) of* Teachers Have It Easy: The Big Sacrifices and Small Salaries of America's Teachers. *She is also the co-founder of The Teacher Salary Project and producer of the film* American Teacher.

**Mariama Lockington** *is an associate editor of* Be Honest *and the programs coordinator for 826 National. Originally from Michigan, she moved to Oakland after earning a B.A. in creative writing and African American studies from the University of Michigan. Prior to working at 826, Mariama completed a two-year teaching fellowship with Citizen Schools, where she taught writing to middle school students around the Bay Area. She recently received a master's degree in education from Lesley University and is a published poet.*

**Laura McKinney** *is an associate editor of* Be Honest. *She has dedicated her life to empowering youth through volunteerism, global education, art, and writing. Laura received a B.A. in English literature with a minor in anthropology from Mills College and has worked with many youth organizations both abroad and in the San Francisco Bay Area. She was first published at age seventeen in 826 Valencia's 2003 book* Talking Back: What Students Know About Teaching.

# About 826 National

## 826's MISSION

826 National is a network of nonprofit organizations dedicated to helping students, ages six through eighteen, with expository and creative writing, and to helping teachers inspire their students to write. 826 chapters are located in San Francisco, Los Angeles, New York, Chicago, Ann Arbor, Seattle, Boston, and Washington, D.C. Our mission is based on the understanding that great leaps in learning can happen with one-on-one attention and that strong writing skills are fundamental to future success. We offer innovative and dynamic project-based learning opportunities that build on students' classroom experience and strengthen their ability to express ideas effectively, creatively, confidently, and in their own voices.

Each 826 chapter offers after-school tutoring, field trips, workshops, and in-school programs—all free of charge—for students, classes, and schools. We target students in public schools, particularly those with limited financial, educational, and community resources.

## 826's HISTORY

826 Valencia opened its doors in 2002, growing out of a desire to partner the professional literary and arts community of San Francisco with local students in need of engaging learning opportunities.

The tutoring and writing center was designed to be a vibrant setting for rigorous educational activities. Connecting students with local authors, artists, and college students while providing a space that is whimsical and fun proved to be an excellent model for achieving results, and the idea was replicated in seven additional cities.

Since 2004, 826 chapters have opened in Brooklyn, Los Angeles, Chicago, Seattle, Ann Arbor, Boston, and most recently, Washington, D.C., each with a unique storefront as the gateway to the writing center. While the theme of each center is varied (in Los Angeles students are encouraged to dabble in time travel, while in Chicago they may begin their careers as future spies), the 826 model always holds true: if you offer students rigorous and fun learning opportunities and one-on-one attention, they will make great strides in their writing skills and confidence.

As the 826 model spread, the flagship center was home to the nationwide support of the individual chapters, determining and encouraging the use of shared best practices, setting standards for program evaluations to ensure the quality of 826 programming, and framing the national dialogue about the work of teachers and the value of teaching writing. In 2004, the legal name of 826 Valencia was changed to 826 National, to reflect this bigger-picture work. Meanwhile, in San Francisco the programs continued to grow bigger and stronger. In 2008, we made the decision to formally separate into two legal entities to reflect the different initiatives of the local San Francisco chapter and the national one. As of July 2008, 826 National exists as its own legal entity, apart from 826 Valencia, and supports the individual 826 chapters across the nation.

Pirette McKamey, the teacher with whom 826 Valencia worked at Mission High School in 2009, said this about our collaboration: "When students work with people one-on-one on their writing, the benefit is so great. It helps students begin to recognize the relationship between their writing and communication to other people—that writing actually has the power to do that. It's great to have outside people. I think the students feel less comfortable working with outside people, so they have to do some self-struggle and overcome barriers to figure out how to communicate their ideas to someone they don't assume is sympathetic. And it's good for them—very powerful, and good for them."

## OUR STUDENT PROGRAMMING

Each year, 826 is able to provide 25,000 students from low-income families and low-performing school districts with one-on-one tutoring, writing instruction, classroom support, and a wide variety of publishing opportunities. We provide students with high-quality, engaging, and hands-on literary programming. The result: better writing, improved grades, stronger community ties between young people and professional adults, and brighter futures.

All eight 826 chapters offer the following:

*After-school tutoring:* Neighborhood students receive free one-on-one tutoring five days a week in all subject areas at each center. 826 National's tutoring program is designed to inspire learning, foster creativity, and help students understand and complete their homework each day. We accomplish this by providing youth—particularly low-income youth, including those who live near our locations—free access to invaluable academic assistance.

*Workshops:* Our free workshops foster creativity and strengthen writing skills in a variety of areas. All offerings directly support classroom curriculum while engaging students with imaginative and often playful themes. Workshops are project-based and taught by experienced, accomplished literary professionals. Examples or topics include: "Writing for Pets" (just what it sounds like!); "Mad Science," in which students, wearing lab coats, isolate strings of their own DNA and then write stories about their DNA mutating in strange ways; "How to Persuade Your Parents, Or: Whining Effectively"; "Spy Training"; and "How to Write a Comic Book," taught by a professional cartoonist.

*Publishing:* 826 publishes an array of student-authored literary quarterlies, newspapers, books, chapbooks, and anthologies, which are displayed and sold in the retail shops that front our writing centers and are distributed and sold nationwide. We use professional editors and designers to allow the students' work to shine. Our most significant student collaboration each year, the Young Authors' Book Project, partners a local high school classroom with professional writers and editors. The students spend three to four months crafting essays around a particular theme, continually collaborating with adult tutors through the editing and publishing process. When the project is complete, we celebrate the release with a festive party. The final book is a stunning reflection of months of hard work, engagement, and dedication on the part of the students and tutors.

*Field trips:* Up to four times a week, 826 chapters welcome an entire public school classroom for a morning of high-energy learning. In one field trip, "Storytelling & Bookmaking," students write, illustrate, and bind their own books within a two-hour period. This is a very popular experience and requires students to work together to develop an original story. They create characters, decide those characters' greatest wish and greatest fear, develop a plot as a group, and then they each write their own conclusion unraveling the tied-up pieces of the story. The students also add a personal touch by gluing their own photos and writing their own author bios on the back cover. By the end of the morning, the young writers have a finished product in hand—tangible proof of their hard work and creativity to show to parents and friends.

*In-schools program:* We dispatch teams of volunteers into local, high-need public schools to support teachers and provide one-on-one assistance to students as they tackle various writing projects, such as school newspapers, research papers, oral histories, and college entrance essays. We serve five thousand students annually through this deeply meaningful partnership with local schools and teachers.

Our five thousand volunteers make our work possible and our programs free of charge. They are local community residents, many of whom are professional writers, artists, college students, parents, bankers, lawyers, and retirees from a wide range of professions. These passionate individuals are found at our centers throughout the day, sitting side by side with our students after school, supporting morning field trips, and helping entire classrooms of students learn the art of writing. Our volunteers actively connect with youth every day.

If you would like to get involved in programs as a tutor or as a donor, please go to the 826 National website, www.826national.org, to find out more information or visit one of our chapter websites. And, please come and visit the chapter (and its engaging storefront) at the location closest to you:

826 Boston
3035 Washington Street
Roxbury, MA 02119
www.826boston.org

826 Chicago
1331 North Milwaukee Avenue
Chicago, IL 60622
www.826chi.org

826DC
3233 14th Street, NW
Washington, DC 20009
www.826dc.org

826LA EAST
1714 West Sunset Boulevard
Echo Park, CA 90026
www.826la.org

826LA WEST
SPARC Building
685 Venice Boulevard
Venice, CA 90291
www.826la.org

826michigan
115 East Liberty Street
Ann Arbor, Michigan 48104
www.826michigan.org

826NYC
372 Fifth Avenue
Brooklyn, NY 11215
www.826nyc.org

826 Seattle
8414 Greenwood Avenue North
Seattle, WA 98103
www.826seattle.org

826 Valencia
826 Valencia Street
San Francisco, CA 94110
www.826valencia.org

826 National
826 Valencia Street
San Francisco, CA 94110
www.826national.org

# Acknowledgments

We want to especially acknowledge Kathleen for believing in her students, for recognizing they had something meaningful to share, and for inviting us into her eleventh-grade English classrooms many, many years ago. We also want to celebrate Gene and Suzanne Valla, the first investors in this project, for kicking off this enriching and unforgettable opportunity for our young authors. Gene and Suzanne were the first people to believe in this book when it was just and idea. Gene was also one of the first people to believe in 826 Valencia when we first started in 2002. Thank you for the opportunities and for believing in young people.

This book was made possible in large part because of the incredible support of our collaborating teachers. They incorporated our prompts into their already-packed curriculum, worked with students during off-hours, and spent time tracking down students whose pieces needed an extra push: all because they believe in the power of their students' voices and wanted to give them a chance to be recognized in a national arena. These are the kinds of teachers we love best; encouraging, supportive, and inspiring, they have dedicated their time and creativity and have become a part of the 826 family. They are: Scott Eberhardt and Guilan Sheykhzadeh in San Francisco, California; Andy Moinar in Los Angeles, California; Belle Belew, Raquel Brown, and Cindy Pineda in Washington, D.C.;

Molly Dunn, Ellen Sale, Janna Walson in Chicago, Illinois; Michelle Boyle in Boston, Massachusetts; Mia Ellis, Alexandra Wakeman, and Rebecca Sullivan in Seattle, Washington; and Quinn Strassel in Ann Arbor, Michigan.

All around the country, our 826 volunteers were hard at work helping students craft the insightful essays in this book. They are the heart of our organization, donating time and talent to help guide our students through the process of writing and revision. We are astounded and grateful for the never-ending support of the following folks who indeed breathed this book into life. They are:

*Ann Arbor:* Alissa Arden, Mitra Dunbar, Katie Jones, Frances Martin, Jen Trigger Marzullo, and Karen Watts. *Boston:* Kristen Hoggatt, Llewellyn Powell, Megan McManaman, Kit Wallach, Dan Turnbull, Ting Hoepfner, Lauren Leydon Hardy, Megan Gaudet, Abe Gore, Shane Artsy, Maria Pinto, Walter Smelt III, Alicenne Reid, Alyssa Fry, John Campbell, Ashley Pitts, and Anna Hale Wolfe-Pauly. *Chicago:* Carrie Colpitts, Jim Joyce, Cristina Lalli, Jeni Crone, Shama Dardai, Lauren Wetherbee, Hayley Miller, Clare Hiatt, Paul Lask, Jessica Palmer, Laura Perelman, Erica Schwanke, Alyssa Rusak, Steve Klise, Kathryn Spangler, Joshua Ruddy, Mo Gallagher, and Adam Kivel. *Los Angeles:* Samuel Cheney, Jennifer Martinez, Gabby Messineo, Donica Patel, Corey Chan, Ian Besler, Staceey Gerbman, and Ana Haase-Reed. *San Francisco:* Cheryllе Taylor, Hannah Edber, Sarah Allen, Karly Dowling, Jody Owens, Kristen Stotts, Emily Kennedy, and Kathy Taylor. *Seattle:* Kate Jenks, Jeremiah Oshan, Annalisa Concerti-Jones, and Ian Schooley. *Washington, D.C.:* Lucia Graves, Elvira Cooper, Cathy Smith, Ryan Little, Kevin Redmon, Alyssa Work, Sullivan Cousins, Wesley Schantz, Elizabeth Falk, Mariam Al-Shawaf, and Kira Wisniewski;

We thank our dedicated 826 executive directors, Leigh Lehman, Joel Arquillos, Teri Hein, Mara O'Brein, Amanda Uhle, Scott Seeley, Daniel Johnson, Joe Callahan, and Naomi Ayala, for upholding the mission of 826 and supporting teachers and staff in the creation of yet another beautiful and insightful student publication.

Of course, we are deeply indebted to the 826 programming staff—Ryan Lewis, Danny Hom, Bonnie Chau, Julius Diaz Panoriñgan, Kathleen Goldfarb, Kait Steele, Pat Mohr, Amy Sumerton, Lindsey Plait Jones, and Mike Scalise—for their tireless work supporting tutors, collecting essays, encouraging students, and making this project a huge success all around.

We are grateful for encouragement we received from our agent Julie Doughty, and the support of the 826 team: Ryan Lewis, Lauren Hall, Erin Archuleta, and Gerald Richards.

We would also like to thank President Barack Obama, Secretary of Education Arne Duncan, and Sherman Alexie for giving us the inspiration for this book.

As always, we must thank Eli Horowitz for lending his tremendous wisdom to both the original *Talking Back* project and this sequel. His sharp eye and editing expertise were deeply appreciated and we are grateful for his dedication.

And, finally, we are very grateful for the savvy and helpful comments from our editor, Sarah Fan, and to the team at The New Press for giving these students' words the professional platform and audience their work deserves.

—Nínive Calegari, Mariama Lockington, and Laura McKinney